Morton Greats

Morton Greats

Graeme Ross

breedon **books**
PUBLISHING

First published in Great Britain in 2004 by
The Breedon Books Publishing Company Limited
Breedon House, 3 The Parker Centre,
Derby, DE21 4SZ.

I would like to dedicate this book to my dad,
John Ross, a lifelong Morton supporter and to
Jim Simpson who although not a 'Ton fan would
have loved this book.

ISBN 1 85983 436 1

Printed and bound by CROMWELL PRESS,
TROWBRIDGE, WILTSHIRE

Contents

Acknowledgements

As with all books of this type there are many people to thank for their time and co-operation. First of all, the subjects themselves who were all generous with their time, memories and photographs. Sadly, the immortal trio of Campbell, Cowan and Orr are no longer with us, but I was greatly helped by their friends, relatives, opponents and teammates. I am especially grateful to Ronnie Cowan and Ronnie Campbell for helping provide photographs and for sharing their memories of their fathers. Grace Gough of *The Herald*, Roger Graham of the *Greenock Telegraph*, Andy Gemmell, Danny Goodwin and George Ralston were invaluable sources of photographs. I would also like to thank the following for giving the book valuable exposure; Inverclyde Online, the *Greenock Telegraph*, Morton Football Club and Morton Unofficial.net. Others who were happy to help were Bob Crampsey, Noel Davies, Dr Adam Little, Tom Brannigan senior, Allan McMillan and Campbell Thomson of the *Daily Record*, Tom Robertson, David Brown, John Cameron, Margaret Telfer, Neil Orr, Ishbel Orr, and Allister McQuarrie. It would be remiss of me also not to thank Arthur Montford, Douglas Rae, Chris Jewell and Vincent Gillen who all offered sage advice and passed on the benefit of their experience. Then of course there are the many colleagues and opponents of all the players, who were happy to chat about their memories. And final thanks must go to my wife Ann, for her patience, understanding and support, and to Breedon Books for giving me the opportunity to publish the book. Apologies to anyone I have neglected to mention.

Introduction

As Derek Collins says somewhere in this book, there is just something about Morton. Something that goes beyond mere silverware. Supporting a club like Morton is full of highs and lows. Morton fans are not glory hunters. They love their club and they love good football. They also recognize the importance of a football club in a community such as Inverclyde. Under Chairman Douglas Rae, Morton have bounced back from the threat of extinction, and the club has worked hard to foster this community spirit. Over the years Morton fans have forged a special bond with the club and the players, and in 130 years there have been some great Morton players. When I first jotted down the names of my 10 Morton Greats I had a firm 10 in my mind and resolved never to deviate from my chosen elite. I considered the immediate post-World War Two period a good starting-off point, and I wanted to fairly represent the subsequent decades. Therefore the 10 in the book are my original 10, but I must confess that when I looked at some of the players that didn't make the book, I did have second thoughts. For example, how could I leave out the immortal Billy Steel? One of Scotland's greatest-ever players, Billy first made his name at Cappielow, but much of his career at 'Ton was spent overseas in the army, and although he was capped by Scotland and represented Great Britain against the Rest of the World as a Morton player, I felt Campbell, Cowan, and Orr more than adequately represented the fine sides of the immediate post-war years. Longevity was also a key factor in my selection. All of the 10 with the possible exception of Joe Harper had long careers at Cappielow, and I could hardly leave out wee Joe anyway, so proud is he of his Greenock and Morton background. None of Morton's many excellent Scandinavian players made the book either, largely because they were very quickly transferred, but if ability alone had been the sole factor, then Preben Arentoft and Janne Lindberg would have walked into the 10. It was also a wrench to leave out personal favourites like Gerry Sweeney, Davie Hayes, George Anderson, Jim Duffy, Jim Hunter, Neil Orr and Joe Mason, but like a Davie Hayes tackle, I had to be ruthless. I sincerely hope that my choice provokes much debate. I don't claim that my 10 players are Morton's greatest 10, merely 10 of the greatest. So for those of you who are disappointed that your own personal favourite is missing from the book, all I can say is; maybe next time!

Foreword
by Arthur Montford

Arthur Montford is a director of Morton and he has supported the club for over 60 years. He was a journalist for many years and was presenter of *Scotsport*, the longest-running sports show in the world (*Guinness Book of Records*) for over 30 years.

A voyage of nostalgia brings many pleasures and many surprises, and when Morton chairman Douglas Rae and myself spoke to Graeme Ross at the very start of his adventurous journey back through the years in search of the great players who had worn the famous blue and white hoops, we did warn him that it would take him longer than he thought, and suggested to him that his biggest problem would not be deciding who should be included, but rather determining who should be left out.

Graeme's decision to concentrate on Morton players who featured in the teams after World War Two has, I think, been a wise one. You have to start somewhere – even if it means leaving for another day perhaps the club's formative years, the famous Scottish Cup winning side of 1922, and the wartime years that produced the remarkable sight of Stanley Matthews and Tommy Lawton playing in the hoops.

One of the most remarkable and rewarding features of Graeme's meticulous research and diligent trawl through press cuttings, old programmes and the club's archive is the great diversity of players he has written about. Two of the quietest players I ever knew were two of our all time superstars – Billy Campbell of the long stride and beautifully judged tackle, and Jimmy Cowan, prince of goalkeepers, the first name you would put down on any greatest-ever Morton selection. Both were modest men who loved to play in the jersey. Indeed, as many Morton fans know, Jimmy always wore a Morton shirt under his Scottish yellow jersey.

There are many others of course, and like you I am looking forward to turning the pages which await to take a happy trip down memory lane with Graeme who will introduce some of yesterdays heroes to today's fans, along with some more recent stars... surely a labour of love.

Chapter 1

Billy Campbell
All Over the Field

On first viewing Billy Campbell's playing record with Morton, there is very little to support his inclusion in a Morton Hall of Fame. A mere 73 competitive games and six goals over three seasons is hardly the stuff of legend. However, when you add a successful wartime career, 10 Scotland caps, a Scottish Cup runners-up medal, and the glowing tributes of many observers and contemporaries, then an entirely different picture of Billy Campbell begins to emerge. Billy Campbell was part of a generation of footballers whose careers were curtailed by World War Two. Not only did Billy's career suffer because of the war, it was also sadly cut short just when he was reaching his peak, when he contracted TB. These factors go some way to explaining the paucity of appearances in the record books. Billy was the oldest of Morton's celebrated international trio of Campbell, Cowan and Orr. If Cowan was the goalkeeping hero who at times was all that stood between Morton and a thrashing, and Orr was the match-winner, then Billy was the heartbeat of one of Morton's finest-ever sides. His driving displays as a swashbuckling wing-half led Billy to be known as 'All over the field Campbell'.

Billy Campbell was the original local boy made good. He was born in Greenock in 1920, and from an early age was kicking a ball about the streets around his home. Both Billy and his brother showed promise from an early age despite the

Billy Campbell's Morton jersey and Scottish cap.

opposition of their father, who thought that football was a rather silly pastime. Undeterred, Billy played for Greenock schoolboys and the Boys Brigade, and signed for Greenock Bluebell in 1936. He progressed from there to the short-lived junior side Morton Juniors. Billy's elder brother had previously been signed by Morton Juniors, and then been let go, much to the chagrin of the boys' mother, who seems to have taken over the role as her boys' protector. Mindful of this, Mrs Campbell insisted that Billy be given six games to make his mark, which he did. He duly signed for Morton Juniors in 1938. In their short history Morton Juniors made a big impression on the junior game, and reached the Scottish Junior Cup Final in 1940 with Billy in the side. Billy had by now developed into a strong tackling wing-half, and his reputation had begun to grow. So much so, in fact, that when the Morton Juniors manager Jimmy Davies moved up and took over as

Billy Campbell's Scotland jersey and Scottish cap of 1946.

manager of the senior Morton side he took Billy and several other players with him. Billy signed for Morton in 1941, and combined playing with working for local firm Hasties as a turner. The timing might have been unfortunate as regards the Scottish League programme, with the Leagues now regionalised, but Billy had joined a decent Morton side, then playing in the Scottish Southern League. In 1942 for example, the Morton side included five players who had, or were soon to represent Scotland. Billy made an immediate impact in his first season, scoring the winning goal in the semi-final replay of the Southern League Cup at Ibrox against Partick Thistle. A newspaper report of the match described Billy's goal and performance as a rarity for a wing-half at that time, praising his vision and shooting ability. Billy's goal, a 25-yard left-footer, was compared in the *Greenock Telegraph* to Jimmy Gourlay's famous winner in the 1922 Scottish Cup final. Billy almost made it two in the last minute when another shot hit the bar. The *Telegraph* also reported that the Morton fans packed the trains home to Greenock, some of them spending the journey in the luggage racks and guards van. Unfortunately, Morton lost the final of the Southern League Cup, in essence one of the first Scottish League Cups, 1–0 to Rangers.

Billy initially played for 'Ton at left-half, but when centre-half Gray was drafted into the army, right-half Willie Aird was moved to centre-half and Billy was moved, initially as an experiment, to right-half. Billy soon made the position his own, and his impressive displays quickly attracted the Scottish national side selectors. He was included as a travelling reserve for an international match against England at Hampden in April 1943. Wartime international matches were not officially recognised for caps purposes, often including understrength sides, but were immensely popular, lifting the morale of a nation mired in a seemingly endless wartime struggle. Scotland played England again six months later at Maine Road in Manchester, and this time Billy made the starting line up of a

CAMPBELL

rather understrength Scottish side. The same couldn't be said of the English side, however, who had all their big guns out. Billy played at left-half and was powerless to prevent Matthews, Carter, Lawton and the rest from inflicting an 8–0 thrashing on the hapless Scottish side. Dr Adam Little, then of Rangers and later of Morton, was Billy's wing-half partner and recalls, 'Billy and I didn't see the ball twice between us that day.'

It was an unfortunate start to Billy's international career, but he went on to play further unofficial international matches against Wales in 1945, Northern Ireland in 1946, and England in April 1946. He also played in a Scottish representative side in a match to raise funds for the Bolton disaster after 33 spectators were killed when crush barriers collapsed during a match at Burnden Park. At club level Billy and Morton continued to improve. Under the canny management of Jimmy Davies Morton began to build one of their finest-ever sides. The list of players who graced Cappielow in the 1940s includes many of the club's finest-ever players. Initially Archie McFeat was the goalkeeper. McFeat was a more than competent goalie, but once the peerless Jimmy Cowan came on the scene he moved on. At full-back there was a fine combination in Matt Maley and Andy Fyfe, and at left-half the resolute Jimmy Whyte. Billy himself thought the world of 'Banana Fyfe', a fearless full-back. Forwards included the tall, elegant Tommy Orr, and the brilliant left-wing combination of Billy Steel and Johnny Kelly. Steel went on to become one of the most revered Scottish footballers of all time. Signed on a free transfer from St Mirren, he would command a world-record transfer fee of £15,500 when he left Morton for Derby County in 1947. Unfortunately, his skills were denied to Morton for long periods due to service in the army, but he remains a legendary figure at the tail o' the bank. In addition to these players were the wartime 'guests' who played for Morton. Famous players such as Stanley Matthews and Tommy Lawton 'guested' for Morton during the war, and playing with them exerted a vast influence on Billy, who felt he could only really learn through playing with such greats.

Old heads such as ex-Celts Johnny Crum and John Divers also featured, and they attracted large crowds to Cappielow. During the war football was one pleasure that people could still enjoy and Cappielow had average crowds of 8–10,000, with even the likes of Aberdeen attracting 15,000 for one match. There were also unusual diversions to boost morale and distract people from the austerity, such as an evening at the Battery Park in Greenock when ex-Morton and Scotland goalkeeper Harry Rennie appeared at an exhibition. Morton's 1922 Cup Final hero Jimmy Gourlay agreed to try and repeat his winning goal against Rangers with six attempts at goal against Rennie from the same position as the Cup Final goal. Unfortunately there seems to be no record of the outcome. Could it be that the infamous Greenock weather intervened? It would have

A young Billy Campbell (left) with friends.

saved Rennie a fortune, as he had agreed to donate to the POW fund for every goal he lost.

Morton performed well during the war years, and Billy's form kept him in the thoughts of the international selectors. By the time of his second cap in 1945 against Wales at Hampden, this time at right-half, Billy's reputation had been well established. He was the perfect build for a half-back at 5ft 9in, and just under 12 stone. His stamina was legendary. He was quick to support his forwards, but always ready, willing and able to get back to help his defence. He was renowned as a hard but fair tackler, and was generally reckoned to be the best slide tackler in the Scottish game. The sliding tackle was a particular feature of his play, and when he did win the ball, he was loath to follow the example of most half-backs of the time and just lump it anywhere. He always tried to find a teammate with the ball, and generally succeeded. The famous Celtic and Scotland goalkeeper Ronnie Simpson described Billy as a brilliant distributor of the ball and wrote in a newspaper article: 'I have yet to see a half back who can part with a ball like Billy Campbell, and I cannot recall a time when he let Scotland down.'

Billy Campbell

Citing Billy's ability to emerge with the ball even against much heavier opponents, Ronnie also bestowed on Billy the grand title of 'The best tackler in the world.'

During all his success with Morton and Scotland Billy remained a quiet, modest person, quite happy to combine working in Hastie's factory with his football. In fact, he was so quiet that he often had to be ushered to the front of the bus queue as he waited for the bus to take him to Cappielow on match days after he had finished his shift. A different world indeed from today's stars with their fleets of luxury cars! In February 1946 Billy was capped again in a 3–2 victory against Northern Ireland at Hampden, and despite setting up a goal for Jock Dodds, it wasn't quite as happy a memory for him as he picked up an ankle injury and finished the match hobbling out on the right wing. The injury kept Billy off the pitch for a few weeks, but he was fit enough to be named in the Scotland side to face England at Hampden in April 1946. An incredible 140,000 fans turned out to see Scotland triumph 1–0. Although the war had been over for almost a year these matches were not yet designated official internationals, despite both countries having very close to their best sides on display. If there is one match in Billy's career that sums up all of his qualities as a player, then this is the one. The *Greenock Telegraph's* headline read 'Morton's star shone in exciting Hampden international.' The paper went on to say:

In its long association with football Greenock has contributed numerous players who have helped enhance Scotland's soccer reputation, but in

Billy Campbell it has a star who promises to outshine any of the principals of the past.

The *Telegraph* reported that it was impossible to take your eyes off Billy as he carried out the work of two men with his uncompromising tackles – including his trademark slide tackles – his sweeping passes, and his masterful distribution. After the match Stanley Matthews, who of course had played with Billy during the war as a guest of Morton, was quoted as saying: 'The Scots have a winner in Campbell. He is a neat unassuming type of half-back, and gets through a tremendous amount of work.'

Matthews was especially struck by Billy's industry and ability to attack and defend, and one month later Billy was capped again against Switzerland at Hampden. This was his first official cap, but he was substituted midway through the match after sustaining a recurrence of the ankle injury he had picked up against Northern Ireland a few months previously. Billy had to be carried off and the injury limited his appearances in the first official league season after the war.

Billy Campbell in the Scottish team that beat Ireland 3–2 in 1946. He is third left, back row.

Billy lapping the track at Cappielow in 1948.

Billy was certainly not the luckiest of players with regard to his international career, having to be taken off twice through injury, and missing out on other opportunities as a result. His cap total would undoubtedly have been greater but for these injuries. He was a very fair player, but never held back in the tackle, and it was this whole-hearted approach that unfortunately resulted in him being hurt on the field of play.

The end of the war saw the resumption of the League programme in season 1946–47, and Morton, having established themselves as one of the top sides in the country, were elected to the new First Division, or Division 'A' as it was known. Billy was now a regular fixture in the Scotland side, despite fierce competition from a galaxy of wing-half stars of the time. Billy's cap tally becomes even more impressive when one considers the comparative lack of international matches in those days, plus the fact that his rivals included such excellent players as Bobby Evans, Archie McCauley and Alec Forbes. Billy was capped again against Northern Ireland in November 1946 at Hampden, but was then sidelined with a troublesome knee injury that required an operation.

Morton finished a credible sixth in the First Division in season 1946–47, but Billy missed much of that season due to the knee injury, which continued to hamper his progress. He was fully fit by the following season and his inspired play attracted the attention of Manchester United, who were reported to have offered the celebrated winger Jimmy Delaney in exchange for him. Nothing came of it, and Billy devoted all his energies to Morton in a season which proved to be one of the most memorable, if ultimately disappointing, in Morton's history. Billy was an ever-present in Morton's cup run that year, as the club fought their way to the final of the Scottish Cup. Billy gave a series of inspirational performances, beginning with a first round tie at ice-bound Somerset Park. Billy was outstanding as 'Ton eased past Ayr by two goals to one. Falkirk, Queens Park and Airdrie had all been disposed of before 'Ton faced Celtic in the semi-final at Ibrox. Around 80,000 fans witnessed Eddie Murphy score the only goal in extra-time. Morton were through to their first Scottish Cup Final since 1922, and again, as so often in their history, they faced Rangers. Post-war Scotland had thrown off the shackles and austerity of the war years, and football was booming. Incredible crowds were being attracted to matches, and the Morton v Rangers Final on 17 April 1948 was watched by an astonishing crowd of 131,629. The match finished 1–1, and the following Wednesday evening 133,629 fans, a world record for a midweek crowd at the time, witnessed the replay. Sadly for Billy and all those connected with Morton, the team could not emulate their 1922 counterparts and

Campbell in action against Third Lanark at a packed Cathkin Park in January 1949. The Hi-Hi won 1–0.

they lost the tie 1–0 in extra time, despite Billy almost scoring with a brilliant shot in the dying moments. The full Morton side for both the final matches was: Cowan, Mitchell and Whigham, Campbell, Miller and Whyte, Hepburn, Murphy, Cupples, Orr and Liddell.

So Billy ended up with another runners-up medal to add to his Junior and League Cup

The Scottish team put in a spot of ball practice at the Forest Hills Hotel grounds. Delaney has the ball, with (right to left) Brown, Campbell, Gordon Smith, J. Shaw and Waddell in the rear.

ones, but there was some consolation just one week later when he won another cap against Belgium at Hampden. Scotland won 2–0 and the Scotland side also included Jimmy Cowan, who was making his Scotland debut. This match was Billy's fourth appearance at Hampden in 18 days. He had also played for Scotland against England a week prior to the Cup Final. Honours were coming thick and fast for Billy now, and in May 1948 he was named in a Scotland touring party along with Cowan. Billy won his fifth and final official full cap against Switzerland in Berne, and his final cap total would have been six had he not missed the following match against France in unusual circumstances. He had been named in the starting line up, but in the run up to the match Billy burst the toe cap of one of his boots. Incredible as it seems now, this was Billy's only pair. He couldn't take to the field and his place was filled by Sammy Cox of Rangers, who really should have had the decency to loan Billy his boots! Billy also won a Scottish League cap against England in 1948, but events were to take a tragic turn the following year when a much more serious event than a burst boot prevented Billy from winning any more caps in his career.

Billy had begun season 1948–49 in effervescent form, contributing four goals in 18 League matches, and in the absence of Jimmy Whyte he had taken over as captain. However, in October 1948 Morton fans were stunned to discover that Billy had asked for a transfer. The *Greenock Telegraph* reported that although Billy

Campbell is introduced to Field Marshall Montgomery before the Scotland against England match in 1948.

was quite happy at Morton, he realised that a footballer's career was short and financial opportunities were limited at the club. Morton had reluctantly agreed to Billy's request and speculation was rife that he would move for a fee larger than the £15,500 Derby had paid for Billy Steel just a year previously. Aston Villa and Tottenham Hotspur were reported to be preparing to bid for Billy, but before anything could come of their enquiries Billy was diagnosed with tuberculosis, then a much more common and potentially fatal disease. In fact, at around that time the Ministry of Health reported that Greenock was in the grip of a tuberculosis outbreak, which was causing grave problems. Thankfully Billy survived, but he could no longer play football at such a high level. His last match was against Dundee in January 1949, and he scored Morton's only goal from a penalty.

So Billy's playing career was tragically cut by his illness. His whole life had been football, and he was a man who prided himself on his fitness and ability to make lung-bursting runs. To no longer be able to play, and to have to retire while at his peak, was a devastating blow. Morton did their best by him, and sent him to Switzerland to recuperate. A testimonial match against St Mirren at Ibrox in August 1950 attracted 26,000 fans. Many old friends, opponents and colleagues turned out in the match in support of Billy, and after the match Billy presented all the participants with a gift. It was a sad and untimely end to a great career, and a measure of Billy's importance to the club is the fact that Morton, despite the skills of Cowan and Orr, were relegated at the end of season 1948–49, just one year after their Cup Final appearance.

Billy eventually came to terms with his retirement from football. A devoted family man, he later bought a newsagents in the town. He remained a popular and revered figure in the Greenock area. He never lost his passion for the game, and was a regular at Cappielow through the years. He also wasn't one of those old pros who would bang on about the game being so much better in his day, although he always said that the great players of his era would still have been greats in the modern game. As the years progressed Billy acknowleged that skills and fitness had improved, although in a newspaper article in 1994, when commenting on the all-conquering Rangers side of the time, he was of the opinion that his Morton side might not have beaten them, but they certainly wouldn't have been afraid of them.

Towards the end of his life, Billy was accorded the respect he had earned as one of Morton's finest-ever players, but he remained the same modest man he had always been. In March 1994 he was invited by the SFA to the official opening of the refurbished Hampden Park, and met many of the players he had played with and against. He enjoyed rekindling old memories with legends of the Scottish game, many of whom had been his teammates with club and country. If he had one regret about his career, it was that he never played at Wembley, despite facing England three times.

Billy Campbell died in 1994 aged 73. Heartfelt tributes were paid to a man who was the very essence of the maxim, 'the game for the game's sake.' In his playing days he was known as the man who never stole a yard at a throw-in. For Arthur Montford he is one of Morton's best-ever players:

An off-duty
Billy Campbell.

Morton players toast Billy Campbell at his testimonial dinner in 1950.

It is easy to forget how good Billy was. He could easily fit into the modern game because he combined attacking strength with great defensive qualities. I know that Willie Waddell considered him one of the finest wing-halves he had ever played with.

For Bob Crampsey he was 'a cultured wing-half who didn't look out of place in a Scotland side containing greats like Billy Steel and Billy Liddell.' Hibernian's 'Famous Five' inside-left Eddie Turnbull crossed swords on the field with Billy many times, and remembers Billy as 'a very astute player, skilful, with tremendous energy, and superb in the tackle.'

From the day Billy signed for Morton until his last match eight years later, he distinguished himself with his many fine qualities. His mastery of the tackle, stamina, sportsmanship, passing ability and all-round excellence made him one of the most admired half-backs in the British game. It can certainly be argued that if he hadn't been forced to retire he would have won many more caps, and established himself as one of the greats of the Scottish game. He might even have been granted his transfer and moved to a grander stage with a bigger club. But all that is conjecture. It is enough for Morton fans to know that Billy Campbell was one of the finest players and gentlemen ever to grace Cappielow, and to remember him as the quintessential local hero who was proud to serve only one club, his home town club. In short, Billy Campbell was a model professional.

Morton playing statistics: (League, League Cup, Scottish Cup)

Season	Appearances	Goals
1946–47	15	1
1947–48	34	1
1948–49	24	4

Tommy Orr,
1952.

Chapter 2

Tommy Orr
Gentleman Player

In the murky world of modern-day football, where cash is king and agents do their utmost to move players from club to club, it is refreshing to look back to a more Corinthian age when for some players it was enough just to play 'for the jersey.' Tommy Orr was one such footballer. He was one of that increasingly rare breed; a one-club man. Not only that, it was his local club, one he was happy to serve for 16 years. And of course it ran in the family. When Tommy's son Neil showed signs of following in his father's footsteps and becoming a professional footballer, there was only one club he was ever likely to sign for – Morton. Looking back to the 1940s and 50s it is easy to forget the impact that Tommy Orr made on Morton fans. He was a hero to many, a gentleman to everyone who encountered him, and Morton fans even dedicated their own song to him. He is mentioned, along with Jimmy Cowan and Billy Campbell, the other members of Morton's great 1940s triumvirate, in Greenock-born Alan Sharp's acclaimed novel *A Green Tree in Gedde*, which is set in Greenock. If Jimmy Cowan was the talisman, and the 'Prince of Goalkeepers', and Billy Campbell was the driving force of the Morton side, then Tommy Orr was the match-winner, the classic old-fashioned inside-forward who could win the match with one stroke of genius.

Tommy Orr was born in Gourock in 1924, and was an outstanding prospect even as a youngster. He played schoolboy football and represented the rest of Scotland against Glasgow, after which he played a trial with Rangers second IX. Nothing was forthcoming from Rangers, although it wouldn't be the last time they coveted Tommy, and Morton stepped in. He signed provisional forms for Morton in 1940, and played a few matches for Morton Juniors, but before long his precocious talents ensured a regular place in the full Morton side. The war years saw Morton, under the canny Jimmy Davies, assemble a side full of internationals, and Tommy didn't look out of place alongside such terrific players as Billy Steel, Billy Campbell, Johnny Kelly and Johnny Crum. Many Morton fans of a certain vintage will get a trifle misty-eyed as they reel off the names of one of Morton's best-ever forward lines; Adams, Orr, Crum, Steel, and Kelly.

Crum was a wily ex-Celt who had been capped for Scotland in the 1930s. He considered Tommy one of the finest young players he had ever played with, and took great delight in nodding the ball towards him because the youngster was so easy to pick out. Football was the one thing certain to lift the population's spirits during the war, and with Greenock taking such a battering from the Luftwaffe, it took on even greater importance. Although formal league programmes had been suspended, the clubs played in regional cups and leagues and Morton attracted large crowds. There were many excellent and popular players in the side, including Billy Campbell, but in a team full of stars, Tommy Orr stood out. He soon struck up a great rapport with the equally precocious Billy Steel. They were like chalk and cheese off the park, with Steel so sure of himself and his talent, whereas Tommy was, and would remain, supremely modest and self-effacing. On the park, however, on the sadly too few occasions they played together, they were a joy to watch. In 1942 Morton reached the Southern League Cup Final where the following side lost 1–0 to Rangers: McFeat, Maley and Fyfe, Campbell, Aird and Whyte, Cumner, Orr, Hunter, Steel and Kelly.

Tommy was just 18 years old, and for the next two years he wowed the Morton fans with a string of outstanding performances. But just as Tommy's career was taking off the war intervened and Tommy joined the army in 1944. He had attended university and as such he was commissioned into the Royal Artillery as a lieutenant. His training was spent in Norway, but with unfathomable logic he

Morton in 1947. Orr is second from left, front row.

was then posted to Burma! While serving in Burma he saw frequent action and was lucky to escape with his life on one particular occasion when his unit was ambushed by Japanese snipers. Tommy was awarded several medals for his service during the war, but in common with many veterans he didn't like to talk too much about it, preferring to relate more light-hearted stories about the time his mother sent him a dumpling to celebrate his 21st birthday. By the time the pudding reached Singapore, it was so hard that it was only fit for playing football with! When the war ended Tommy was only 21, but like so many of his contemporaries he had lost some of his best years. And of course, he didn't immediately leave the army at the end of the war. Like Jimmy Cowan it was not until 1947 that he returned full-time to Morton. Yet he had nevertheless made an impression at Morton during the war. He would periodically return home on leave and turn out for the club. In one match against Hamilton Accies, the famous English goalkeeper Frank Swift was guesting for the opponents. Tommy scored with a penalty in the first half with his right foot and was then injured, although he played on regardless. In the second half Morton were awarded another penalty and, unperturbed, Tommy coolly converted it with his left foot. This was a perfect example of the man's two-footed ability, and also his coolness under pressure. According to Bob Crampsey Tommy exuded a marvellous calm, and always seemed to know what his next move was:

> *Tommy was a very tall lean man, taller than the average inside-forward. He was no greyhound, but he was a very intelligent player. In the Morton side of the forties he was the quiet man in contrast to the more ebullient Billy Steel, but he was never overawed.*

Tommy Orr and Rangers and Scotland skipper George Young pay a visit to a children's ward prior to a Scotland match in 1952.

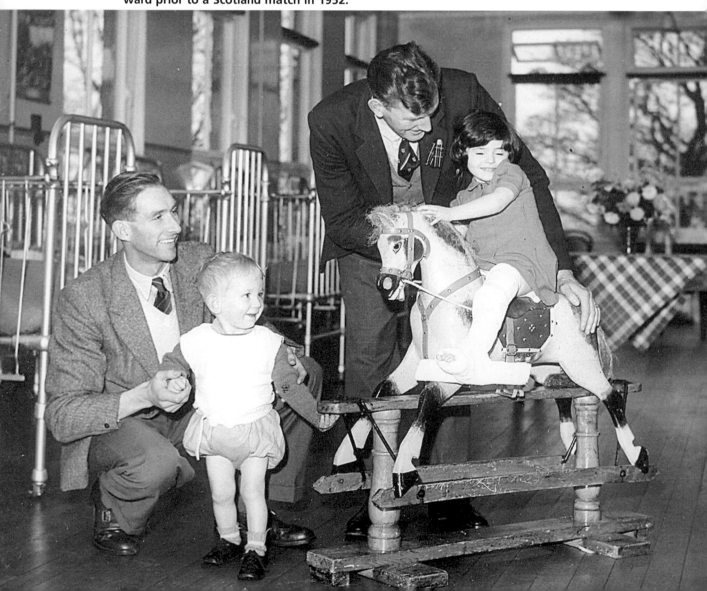

Photographs of Tommy in his playing days show how tall and slim he was. He had a long, rangy stride which allowed him to traverse the infamous Cappielow mud. For many fans, their memories of Tommy are of him striding through the mud on a mazy run and finishing off with a long-range shot which more often than not ended in a goal. He was also adept at conducting play, his natural two-footed ability allowing him to ping passes to either side of the park. He always seemed to make space for himself, and always had time on the ball, and was also very strong in the air.

Readers of the *Greenock Telegraph* were kept well informed with regard to Tommy's military service. The edition dated 25 March 1946 carried the report that Tommy had been promoted to the rank of captain. Tommy was, of course, still playing football during his service and he represented the army side on several occasions. After his military service ended Tommy rejoined Morton as the Scottish League resumed its normal programme. The first season after the war, 1946–47, was a washout for many players, Tommy included. He only managed two league matches. The following season, however, was one of the finest of his career, as Tommy settled back into the form that had made him such an admired and sought-after player during the war. One of his most memorable performances that season was against Celtic at Cappielow.

It was a typical mud-splattered match at Morton's now infamous mud bath, which doubled as a football park. This match more than any other accounts for many fans' image of Tommy ploughing through the Cappielow mud. He was outstanding as Morton thrashed Celtic 4–0, and scored twice. His second was a typical Tommy Orr goal – a mazy run past two players, topped off by an unstoppable shot. In 1947–48 Tommy was arguably at the peak of his powers and recorded his best-ever goals total for a season with 18 strikes. He was a key player for Morton in their march to the Scottish Cup Final that season. Tommy played a large part in 'Ton reaching the final with goals in early rounds against Falkirk and Airdrie, scoring the winner against Falkirk at Cappielow. After the Falkirk match Waverley of the *Daily Record* demanded that Tommy be included in the next Scottish international side. Comparing Tommy to the great inside-forwards of the past the *Record's* correspondent wrote:

Tommy Orr and Jimmy Cowan in action for Morton in the 1948 cup final.

He is everything a great inside forward should be. For a man of his size his control is astounding. Thje ball is seldom more than twelve inches from his feet. He dribbles like George Stevenson, has the power of a McPhail and the shot of a Venters.

Unfortunately for Tommy he was injured against Rangers shortly after these remarks, and the international call-up never came. The same injury forced him to miss the semi-final, but against the odds Morton defeated Celtic 1–0 at Ibrox in front of 80,000 fans, thanks to a goal from Tommy's replacement Eddie Murphy. Tommy's injury caused him to miss the four matches leading up to the final itself, but he was deemed fit enough to take his place against Rangers at inside-left. Tommy stood out in the first half with his calm, accomplished play, but his effectiveness was reduced in the second half, when he received a nasty knock. He finished the match limping with a badly bruised foot. Sadly, Morton lost the replay, but both the club and Tommy's reputation had been greatly enhanced, although not sufficiently to earn Tommy a chance to prove himself for the national side.

In the years just after the war, Scotland had a proliferation of talented inside-forwards. A measure of how well off Scotland were in this respect was the fact that Jimmy Wardhaugh, one-third of Hearts' 'Terrible Trio' of Conn, Bauld and Wardhaugh, was only awarded two caps, despite the fact that he was one of the most prolific goalscorers in the history of Scottish football.

Tommy was equally at home in either inside-forward berth, but faced stiff opposition in the forms of such alumni as Jimmy Mason of Third Lanark and Bobby Johnstone and Eddie Turnbull, two-fifths of the renowned Hibernian 'Famous Five'. Arguably the greatest of them all, Tommy's former Morton teammate Billy Steel, whom Tommy greatly admired, had the inside-left berth tied up, and he was a permanent fixture, winning 30 caps and scoring 22 goals.

Tommy went to America in 1949 on a tour but he was injured, and had to wait until 1951 for his two caps. The first, in October, was against Northern Ireland in the Home International Championship at Windsor Park, when Tommy replaced

Tommy Orr with the ball at his feet.

the injured Billy Steel who, after he had left Morton for a world-record fee of £15,500 in 1947, had established himself as one of the most brilliant and charismatic footballers in the British game. Such was Steel's importance and reputation, that the Scottish selectors took the unprecedented step of taking the injured Steel to Northern Ireland regardless, allowing him until almost the last minute to prove his fitness. The importance of Steel and the Home International Championship itself was highlighted by the ring of secrecy surrounding his fitness. This provoked an outraged Waverley of the *Daily Record* to claim that 'the waiting of the pleasure of Mr Steel is another of the reasons why some professional footballers are given an exaggerated opinion of their own importance.' The insinuation was that Steel had talked the selectors into taking him to Belfast even though he knew he wouldn't be fit, so that he could claim the £20 match fee. An equally outraged Steel refuted these accusations in a newspaper column after the match, and proclaimed himself delighted by his good friend Tommy Orr's outstanding performance.

Waverley had expressed the hope that the 'sensitive' Tommy would not be affected by the uncertainty. The *Record's* man need not have worried, as Scotland won 3–0, and Tommy, playing at inside-left, scored the opening goal, swerving past Irish skipper Roy Vernon and finishing with a neat left-foot shot from 18 yards. He then came in for some tough treatment from the Irish defenders and was the victim of some eight or nine fouls. But each time Tommy just got up and got on with it, and received great praise for his performance. It was an auspicious debut, and Tommy was picked again the following month against Wales at Hampden, although he was moved to inside-right to accommodate the returning Steel. Unfortunately this match was memorable for the wrong reasons as Scotland played poorly and lost 1–0, with Tommy missing a penalty after only nine minutes, striking the post. He was never capped again, and the suspicion was that his penalty miss was held against him.

Jimmy Cowan also played in both these matches. Jimmy's international career would end a year later, and since those halcyon days, no Morton player has been capped for Scotland. With the benefit of nostalgia, and the aura that surrounds Cowan, Campbell and Orr, it is easy to overlook some of the other terrific players

Morton had during this period in their history. Jimmy Whyte was an inspiring captain, and like Tommy Orr also had a son, Jim, who had a fine career in Scottish football. Colin Liddell, the powerful left-winger in the cup final side, later moved to Hearts and Rangers, and full-back Jimmy Mitchell was sold on to Aberdeen for a substantial fee. One of the characteristics of the 1948 cup final side was the excellent team spirit and keen bond between the players. After home matches several members of the side would meet up with their wives in Gourock's Bay Hotel.

When Tommy belatedly won his two caps he was playing some of the finest football of his career. A match against Celtic in September 1951 is often cited as one of the finest performances of his footballing life. It was a League Cup sectional match against Celtic at Cappielow, a game Morton had to win by three clear goals in order to qualify for the quarter-finals. A huge crowd of 22,000 packed Cappielow and there were sporadic outbursts of violence on the terracing as Tommy displayed all his superb ability, scoring both goals in a 2–0 victory. The *Greenock Telegraph* roundly condemned the violence while eulogising about Tommy's performance: 'Tommy Orr was in a class by himself with his mazy runs, dynamic finishing, and strong forceful play. His performance will be recalled for years to come.'

Tommy's second goal was a quintessential Tommy Orr goal. He ran onto a through ball, chipped the ball over a defender and volleyed a tremendous shot past the Celtic goalkeeper. Shades of Gazza in Euro '96! Unfortunately 'Ton couldn't get the third goal they needed, but Tommy's form at last earned him a Scotland call-up.

As Tommy approached 30, Morton's fortunes began to fade, and they were relegated in 1952. For the rest of Tommy's career the club were in the second division. Jimmy Cowan moved to Sunderland in 1953, and Tommy remained one of the last links to the cup final side. By this time Morton were a fairly mediocre team and Tommy stood out. He was still a good player, and deserved a better stage, but he was happy to remain at Cappielow where he was still the fans' favourite. Tommy would make the headlines for the most innocuous of reasons, such as being 'first footed' by a fireman on New Years day when his chimney caught fire.

However, it was always felt that Tommy would eventually move on. After all, Morton were a selling club who inevitably sold most of their stars. Spurs had coveted Tommy for several seasons, and in 1949 he actually turned down the chance to join them. Newcastle were keen and Rangers were always interested, and it appears that Tommy did have the chance to move to Ibrox. Adam Little, a teammate of Tommy's, remembers accompanying Tommy to Ibrox one evening for signing talks:

> *Tommy left the Ibrox boardroom convinced he was about to become a Rangers player. For whatever reason, it never happened. Whether Morton were looking for more money or not, I don't know. But nothing ever became of it, and I never felt Tommy was quite the same player afterwards.*

Some observers feel that Tommy's quiet nature possibly prevented him from realising his true potential, as Arthur Montford recalls: 'Tommy was extremely shy. He was a gentleman on and off the park. Perhaps if he had a bit more of the devil in him, he would have been an even better player.'

Lawrie Reilly said of Tommy:

> *I went on tour with Tommy to America in 1949, and I played with him for Scotland when he won his two caps. Tommy Orr was a hell of a good player to have in your side. He was good on the ball, and excellent in the air, but he was such a quiet lad. In fact, two of the quietest players I have ever known both played for Morton – Jimmy Cowan and Tommy. I felt that Tommy was too quiet, and possibly lacking in confidence, and that may have cost him more caps. But I was proud to have played with both Tommy and Jimmy.*

Noel Davies, son of Tommy's manager at Cappielow, Jimmy Davies, concurs:

> *Oh, Tommy was very quiet. Tommy and Billy Campbell, sometimes you*

would be hard pushed to get a word out of them. Off the field Tommy was an intelligent man, who had been to University. He was a qualified civil engineer who worked with Greenock firm Baird Brothers, so football wasn't the be all and end all for him. He didn't have to depend on it for a living.

Ian MacMillan (the Wee Prime Minister) came up against Tommy many times for Rangers and Airdrie:

Tommy Orr definitely deserved more caps. In those days with so many outstanding inside-forwards it was difficult to get into the Scotland team and stay there. Possibly Tommy didn't get the breaks he deserved. But he was an outstanding player. He had good vision, he was a good passer, he could take a man on, and he worked hard. He had all the attributes a top class inside-forward needed. He also had a good strike rate, he was always looking to score goals. He was also very clever on the ball, and could judge the weight of a pass so that the receiving player didn't need to break his stride.

Tommy frequently found Hibernian's Eddie Turnbull as his direct opponent, and Eddie still remembers their tussles. 'Tommy was a great team player. He really had it all. He could pass, he had good vision and he scored goals. I very much enjoyed playing against him.'

Tommy's last six seasons were spent in the second division as Morton's status in the Scottish game dwindled. He became the elder statesman of the side, and was a great influence on the younger players. At times, he was obviously carrying the side, but Tommy still played with the same dignity and aplomb he had always displayed, and the fans loved him for it.

As Tommy approached his mid-thirties retirement loomed. Tommy played his last League game for Morton on 30 April 1958 against Stranraer. Morton lost 3–1 and Tommy predictably scored their goal.

After retirement Tommy continued to work with Baird Brothers and remained a

Tommy Orr
training with
Scotland in 1951.

popular figure in the area. He became a keen golfer, and was also a useful cricket batsman. A man of many talents, he was even an accomplished pianist. Above all, he was very much a family man and he always put their needs first.

Tommy Orr sadly died, still a young man, in 1973, aged only 49, when he suffered a fatal heart attack while changing a car tyre. Tommy never had the pleasure of following his son Neil's successful football career. He never experienced the pride of watching Neil wear the blue and white hoops that he himself had graced for 16 years. Neil Orr made his first-team debut for Morton in 1976 aged 17. The similarities in style between father and son were obvious for all to see. Both were tall and slim, and Neil had inherited the long, loping style of play that his father had been known for. Neil was stronger in the tackle, however, and as such made his name with Morton as a central defender. It was only later in his career with West Ham and Hibernian that Neil moved further forward into midfield. At Morton, Neil won seven Scottish Under-21 caps and a League cap, and many observers feel that he should have emulated his father and won a full cap. Neil left Morton for West Ham after over 200 games in 1981 for a fee of £350,000, a club record that was only broken in 1997 when Derek Lilley moved to Leeds for £500,000. The famous *Daily Record* journalist Alex 'Candid' Cameron made great play at the time of the fact that Morton had been saved from going bust by selling their best player. The Orr family tree had come full circle. For the last five years of his career Tommy had virtually carried Morton, and was undoubtedly the best player they had in a sea of journeyman professionals, and now, thanks to his son, Morton were placed on a sound financial footing.

The *Greenock Telegraph* paid a warm and moving tribute to Tommy. The editorial read:

> *Nowadays a host of big time footballers are footloose fellows. They move from club to club for financial benefit and no one can blame them too much for that. Tommy Orr was of a different kind. He played schools football in his own home territory, went to Morton Juniors and signed for Morton. He did not seek to go further afield. Nevertheless, he won a high place in the game in Scotland and played for his country. He was wise in*

days that were less lucrative to retire early. In other words he left football before football left him. Tommy showed no regret at exchanging the game for the less spectacular business of civil engineering. He was in short a man of character and quality.

On the second tee at Gourock Golf Club there is a bench with a plaque dedicated to Tommy. It reads simply 'Thomas B. Orr, Sportsman, 1924–1973'. It is a fitting tribute to a modest, understated, but supremely talented man, one who can truly be remembered as a 'Morton Great'.

Morton playing statistics: (League, League Cup, Scottish Cup)

Season	Appearances	Goals
1946–47	2	1
1947–48	36	18
1948–49	30	5
1949–50	34	11
1950–51	29	15
1951–52	30	13
1952–53	13	4
1953–54	32	3
1954–55	25	16
1955–56	42	7
1956–57	38	11
1957–58	29	4

Chapter 3

Jimmy Cowan
The Prince of
Goalkeepers

It is no exaggeration to say that Jimmy Cowan is Morton's greatest-ever player. Jimmy played in an age when caps were not won as freely as today. His 25-cap Scottish goalkeeping record was for many years a record for a Scottish goalkeeper, and was only beaten by Bill Brown in 1966. From 1948–52 Jimmy was Scotland's undisputed number one goalkeeper, and to this day the 1949 England–Scotland Home International is known as 'Cowan's match.' Despite the jokes about Scottish goalkeepers, Scotland have had their fair share of top-class goalies, and Jimmy Cowan must rank as one of the very best, if not the best. Indeed, shortly before his death, when Billy Bremner listed his all-time Scotland side, his goalkeeper was none other than Jimmy Cowan. Although Paisley born and bred he was Morton through and through, and the Morton fans took him to their hearts. Jimmy always wore a Morton blue and white hooped jersey under his goalkeeper's jersey when playing for Scotland, and his first question after 'Cowan's match' was 'What was the Morton score?' (club football was played as normal during the Home Internationals in those days). When told that Morton had won, he simply replied, 'A great day'.

James Cowan was born in Paisley in 1926. As a youngster he played for Mossvale YMCA and John Neilson School. Although he harboured a desire to play as a winger, and also played centre-forward, Jimmy's ability between the sticks was evident from an early age, and he represented Paisley and District Schoolboys aged 14. He came to the attention of his local senior side St Mirren, and signed for them as an amateur in 1942, aged 16. Unfortunately for Jimmy and St Mirren, things did not quite work out, and just like Billy Steel before him, Morton picked him up on a free transfer in May 1944. The circumstances of Jimmy's signing were unusual to say the least. Noel Davies, the son of Morton manager Jimmy Davies, was playing in an amateur match at Paisley's Racecourse playing fields. At half-time Noel's goalkeeper teammate told him that during the match he had been speaking to a spectator who had told him he was Jimmy Cowan and had played for St Mirren. Noel takes up the story:

I remembered Jimmy from a match against Morton when he was with St Mirren. I knew my father was looking for a goalie, so, I arranged for Jimmy to meet me at the end of the match and I asked him if he was playing with anyone. He told me that St Mirren had given him a free transfer, and he had just finished a month's trial with Falkirk and they had freed him too. When I told my father that Jimmy was available, he went up to Paisley the very next day and signed him.

Jimmy Davies was a sound judge of a player, and he obviously saw something in Cowan that no one else at St Mirren or Falkirk could see. But for Jimmy there were more pressing matters than football to consider, and one month later in June

Jimmy Cowan, who played almost 200 games for Morton.

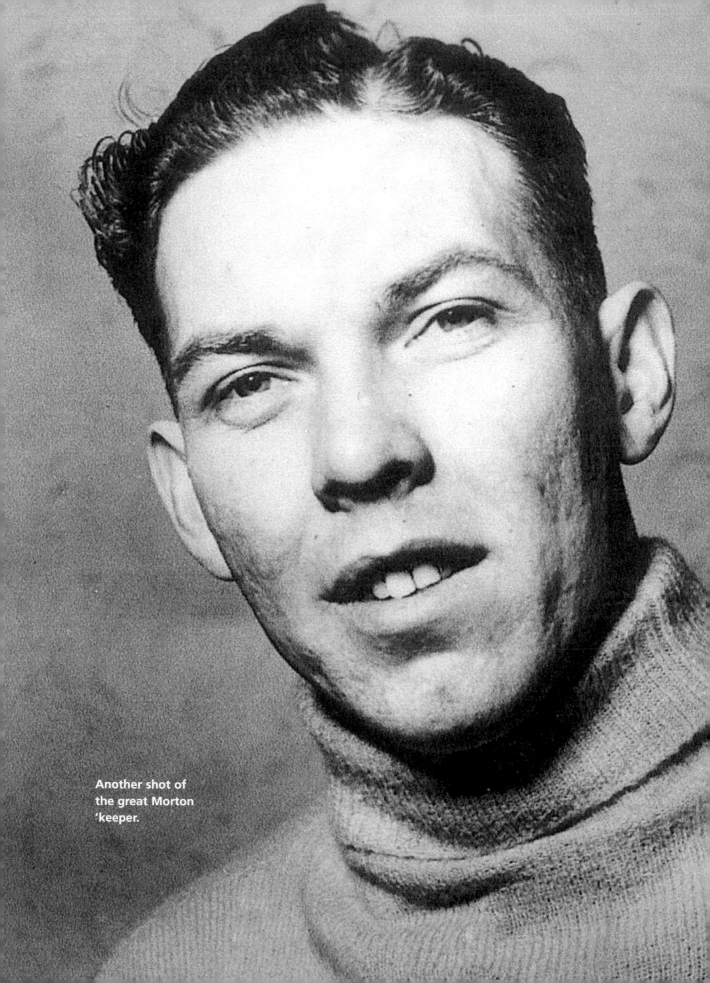

Another shot of
the great Morton
'keeper.

1944, having just turned 18, Jimmy enlisted for the army and any thoughts of a career with Morton were put on hold. Jimmy never liked to talk about his war service. He may well have witnessed things that stayed with him for the rest of his life. Still only just 19 when the war ended, Jimmy must have been profoundly affected by his wartime experience. Certainly, his son Ronnie tells of family holidays when it was a ritual for Jimmy to stop the family car at the Commando memorial at Spean Bridge. What we do know for sure about Jimmy's army service is that he served with the Scots Guards for two years, ending his time with the rank of Lance Corporal. He served in Denmark, and was involved in the liberation of that country from the Nazis. Jimmy was transferred to the Army Physical Training Corps in June 1946, by which time he was a fully fledged Morton player. In a letter from the Scots Guards Headquarters to Ronnie Cowan dated October 1999, Jimmy's conduct while with his regiment is described as 'exemplary'.

During his war service Jimmy played for the British Army, and earned rave reviews for his performances as well as the nickname 'Tiger' Cowan. His reputation travelled as far as Wembley Wizards' goalkeeper Jack Harkness, then writing a column for the *Sunday Post*. Jack telephoned Jimmy Davies and enthused about Cowan, telling Davies that he had a brilliant goalkeeper on his hands.

Army life played havoc with competitive football and Jimmy didn't make his Morton league debut until January 1947 when on weekend leave from the army. That match against Hibs at Easter Road became part of the folklore of Jimmy Cowan, as he made an immediate and memorable impact by saving two penalties. The second penalty came when the 90 minutes were up, and Jimmy pulled off a breathtaking diving save from the famous Gordon Smith and earned Morton a point. The headlines in the evening newspapers proclaimed regular goalie Archie McFeat as the hero, partly due to manager Jimmy Davies reading his team out prior to the match, and through force of habit naming McFeat in goal. The error was soon rectified in the press the following day, and Jimmy was eventually given due recognition for his heroics. Incredibly, the Hibs match was Jimmy's only appearance that season, as he had to return to the army. Jimmy had come into the Morton side at a fortuitous time, for under the astute management of Jimmy

Davies, the club had assembled a side with great potential. There was the famous Billy Steel, one of Scotland's finest ever inside-forwards, also ironically signed from fierce local rivals St Mirren, and the skilful Tommy Orr. And there was Billy Campbell, the driving force of the side, and ex-Celtic star John Divers, who doubled as player-coach. Steel, however, was in dispute with the club over wages and he was transferred to Derby County in late 1947 for a world-record transfer fee. The timing was unfortunate as Morton reached the cup final that season. Who knows what they could have achieved with the brilliant Steel in the side?

Jimmy left the army and returned to Morton in November 1947, going straight back into the side. Almost immediately he began to attract great praise and attention with his performances, and with Morton boasting other excellent players such as skipper Jimmy Whyte, Morton reached the 1948 Scottish Cup Final, thanks in no small measure to Jimmy's performances. The outstanding left-wing combination of Steel and Kelly had been sold to English clubs, but suitable replacements had been found, and Morton were beginning to realise their potential. Jimmy had modelled his game on legendary Scottish goalkeeper Harry Rennie, who had also coached him. It was Rennie who taught Jimmy the practice of marking a line from the centre of the goal to the penalty spot. This allowed Jimmy to have a greater awareness of his positioning and angles, but was frowned upon by officials and groundsmen alike, and was soon outlawed, especially when an over-zealous Airdrie groundsman took it upon himself to mark the line with white paint so as to save his hallowed turf! Jimmy also worked on his own game with some rather unconventional methods. For example, he would often be found on the Clyde coast beaches throwing a ball against large rocks and diving at the rebound.

The 1948 Cup Final against Rangers is remembered for the huge crowds it attracted over two matches. In the first match 131,629 spectators witnessed a 1–1 draw between the two sides. Morton scored through skipper Jimmy Whyte in only the third minute of the match, only for Rangers to equalise five minutes later. Thereafter Morton outplayed their more illustrious opponents, and really should have won the match, forcing 11 corners to Rangers' two. In extra-time alone they hit the woodwork no less than three times. This match also saw one of Jimmy's famous 'miracle saves' after he was caught out of position when a Morton defender pushed the ball back towards his own goal. Jimmy prevented a certain goal by displaying lightning reactions and great agility. As the ball edged closer to the goal line, gathering momentum in the famous Hampden swirl, Jimmy threw himself back acrobatically towards the goal and scooped the ball off the line. This was just one of many fine saves in the two matches, with Jimmy totally dominating his goal area. The replay attracted 133,570 fans, for many years a world-record attendance for a midweek match. Prior to the kick-off, as the players lined up, Jimmy Cowan's common touch was evident once more when a young boy left the packed Morton West terracing and jumped onto the park. He raced towards Jimmy, carrying with him a large wooden imitation of the Scottish Cup. He was stopped by a police sergeant before he could present it to Jimmy, and was

Cowan in typical action diving bravely at the feet of a Celtic forward in 1949.

marched away. But Jimmy had noticed and sprinted after the two, and the boy was allowed to hand the gift to Jimmy as the crowd roared their approval and roundly booed the sergeant.

The replay was again a tight affair, with Jimmy producing several spectacular saves. Rangers eventually triumphed 1–0 in extra-time thanks to a Billy Williamson goal in the gathering gloom. (No floodlights in those far-off days.) After the match there were claims that Jimmy had been momentarily blinded by the flashlights from photographers' flashbulbs at the moment of the goal, but Jimmy typically played them down. However, just prior to the goal the referee had warned a photographer behind Jimmy's goal after Jimmy had almost dropped the ball after being blinded by a flash. The Cup Final was as close as Jimmy came to winning major silverware with Morton. The club, surprisingly since they boasted what many observers feel to be one of their finest sides, were relegated the following season. To his credit Jimmy publicly declared that he was as much to blame as anyone for the relegation and he vowed to do his utmost to return Morton to the top division. This was achieved the following season and Morton returned to the 'A' division as champions.

The Cup Final had thrust Jimmy into the spotlight and the Scottish national team selectors could no longer deny his claim to a cap. He was back at Hampden one week after the replay, winning his first cap in a friendly against Belgium. Scotland won 2–0 in front of 70,000 fans, with Jimmy distinguishing himself with several fine saves. His Morton teammate Billy Campbell was also prominent at right-half. It was the start of a tremendous international career, during which Jimmy was the undisputed number one.

Jimmy sealed his position as Scotland's top goalkeeper in 1949 when he starred in the match that would forever be known as 'Cowan's match'. Scotland travelled down to Wembley to face England in the traditional Home International tournament. It was the most important match in the calendar for many Scottish football fans, and they travelled down to London in their hordes including several hundred from Greenock and district, who were no doubt there to cheer Jimmy and Billy Steel in particular. England were hot favourites, having lost only one match since the war. They boasted a forward line of Matthews, Mortenson, Milburn,

Pearson and Finney, a mouthwatering combination. Both countries had easily beaten Wales and Nothern Ireland, so the match was set up perfectly as the Home International Championship decider, a tremendous prize in those days. Dr Adam Little, then of Rangers and later a teammate of Jimmy's at Morton, was at the match and remembers: 'Jimmy put up the shutters in the first 30 minutes. He made some fantastic saves and broke the hearts of the English forwards.'

Indeed he did. Time and time again Jimmy dived bravely at the feet of the England forwards. One famous photograph shows Jimmy hurling himself at the feet of an English player to block the ball, his blue and white hooped Morton jersey clearly visible under his Scotland goalkeeper's jersey. Jimmy made at least half a dozen fantastic saves in the first half hour, totally demoralizing the English forwards, and instilling tremendous confidence in his own teammates. Scotland won the match 3–1, and Newcastle's famous centre-forward Jackie Milburn was

More action from 1949. Cowan is chaired from Wembley by victorious Scottish fans after their 3–1 win.

one of the English forwards who suffered at the hands of Cowan that day. Years later Jackie recalled just how brilliant Jimmy was against him. 'Jimmy saved at least three shots of mine which I imagined would go past him, and I suspected he knew precisely where the ball was going to before it even left my foot.'

The celebrated Preston North End winger Tom Finney, the man who Bill Shankly thought the best player ever, played on the left wing and was one of the many frustrated Englishmen that day. Interviewed by the author, Sir Tom recalled:

Jimmy Cowan had an outstanding match. He, more than anyone that day, was responsible for Scotland's victory. Some of Jimmy's saves were breathtaking. I remember playing against Jimmy in several England–Scotland matches and he was always top class, but in 1949 he was simply wonderful. Of course this was in the days before players moved about between clubs as much, and played more for the love of the game, and Jimmy was that type of person. The England–Scotland matches were a particular highlight of the season for me, because of the crowds, and the fact that the winner usually won the British Championship. I was very sad when they ended.

The famous Rangers captain George Young was Scotland's skipper that day, and he later recalled in his autobiography that the critics who had written Scotland off that day had reckoned without Jimmy Cowan. 'Corky' described Jimmy's performance as the 'greatest display of goalkeeping he had ever seen.' He also recalled how, after the match as the players were getting changed, with some even about to board the team coach, Jimmy wasn't there.

Eventually Jimmy limped in and slumped on a bench with the words, 'Oh Lord, save us from our friends.' Jimmy had been swamped by hundreds of ecstatic Scotland fans at the final whistle and had literally disappeared from view before being carried from the pitch on the shoulders of the delighted Scotland supporters. His brave and inspiring performance had laid the foundations for a famous victory. The *Greenock Telegraph* reported an English scribe exclaiming

'That lad must be Scotland's greatest discovery since penicillin!' Jimmy himself would only remark after the match 'It was a great experience. I wouldn't have liked to have missed it.'

Still aged only 22, Jimmy Cowan had made his mark as a Scottish footballing hero. Even if he had never played another match, he would have been remembered as a football great. The remarkable thing about Jimmy's performance was that he had only just recovered from injury, having suffered a broken arm. When Jimmy and his Scotland teammates arrived back in Scotland after the match, they were greeted by 10,000 people in Glasgow's Central station. The crowd broke through a police cordon to congratulate the players, roaring 'We want Cowan!', completely ignoring, so it is said, another train with Paris's famous *Folies Bergères* on board! But according to Nocl Davies, Jimmy had a little-known incentive for doing well at Wembley. 'Jimmy's mother was very ill around that time, and she was dying. And she always wanted him to do well because St Mirren had let him go.'

Indeed, Jimmy's first port of call on his return to Scotland was Paisley and the hospital where his mother was a patient. There he was besieged by well-wishers and autograph hunters who all wanted to shake the hand that had beaten the English. Jimmy remained unchallenged as Scotland's number one goalkeeper and earned admiration from all quarters not only for his ability, but also for his sportsmanship. After a World Cup qualifying match in Belfast, which Scotland won 8–2, Jimmy, being a fully paid up member of the goalkeeper's union, was the only player to remain on the pitch as he consoled the hapless and broken Irish goalkeeper.

In 1950 the powers that be had decided that the Home International Championships would serve as qualifiers for the World Cup in Brazil in 1950. The SFA had loftily announced that they would only travel to Brazil as British champions, even though the top two would qualify. In the event Scotland only needed to draw against England at Hampden in the final Home International to finish top, but even with Jimmy in goal, they lost 1–0. In the event, Scotland were still invited to the finals, but the SFA high-handedly stuck to their guns and refused to take part. And so Jimmy was denied the chance to play in the World

The Morton team in 1948. Jimmy Cowan is third from left, back row, in his goalkeeper's jersey.

Cup, but given the shambles of Scotland's efforts and preparation in 1954 and 1958 when they did qualify, this may have been no bad thing.

Despite Morton's continual poor showings in the League (they faced a continual battle against relegation), Jimmy's position as Scotland's number one goalkeeper remained unchallenged. In 1950 and 1951 he played in six successive Home Internationals, and passed the existing goalkeeping cap record of 22 against the US in April 1952. In 1951 Jimmy returned to the scene of his greatest match, and was again triumphant as Scotland beat England 3–2. A feature of Scotland matches at this time was the presence of large contingents of Morton fans, home and away. They were often to be heard shouting for Jimmy and also singing Morton's praises.

Jimmy's performances for Morton continued to be quite exceptional. Many older Morton fans recall thinking that they couldn't see Morton being beaten with Cowan in the side. He was up to his old tricks again against Hibs in November 1951 when he again saved a penalty kick from Eddie Turnbull, and received a standing ovation at the end of the match as his performance earned 'Ton a point. He then extended his reputation as a penalty-kick stopper par excellence with a stunning stop from Celtic's Bobby Collins in a match at Cappielow.

Jimmy won his last cap against Sweden in May 1952, and at the end of the 1951–52 season, Morton were again relegated. Now a combination of Morton's lowly position and injuries cost Jimmy his position as Scotland goalie. Jimmy played one season in the second division, but the time was now right for him to move on. Over the years several English clubs had coveted Jimmy's signature, and it was inevitable that he would eventually move elsewhere. In 1953 Jimmy signed for Sunderland for £9,000. It wasn't a huge fee, but it was good money for Morton, and a chance for Jimmy to earn some decent money. It was a wrench for him to leave Cappielow, but he had a family to think of. He had been at Cappielow a long time, and was now increasingly prone to injury. In an international match against Wales he had damaged his cruciate ligament, and his agility and kicking had been affected. Jimmy stayed two years at Sunderland, and impressed everyone with his qualities, both professional and personal. He left Sunderland in 1955. He was only 29, but injuries had taken their toll. Back in Scotland he helped out Third Lanark briefly, playing six games. His last match was for Third Lanark on 2 January 1956 against Queens Park.

On retiring from football Jimmy trod the well-worn path of the ex-footballer, and went into the licensed trade, taking over a pub in Greenock just yards from where former teammate Billy Campbell ran a newsagent. His pub was adorned with memorabilia from his illustrious career, and he enjoyed reminiscing with customers. He was never entirely at ease with his revered status, and his son Ronnie thinks that he found the whole fame thing quite hard to deal with. Basically, he wanted to move on as he had other interests in his life, his family being his main consideration. Towards the end of his life Jimmy was in poor health. He died at the age of 42 in June 1968. By supreme irony his death occurred on the day it was announced that his beloved Morton had been allocated a place in the Fairs Cities Cup (later the UEFA Cup) – the first and only time Morton have qualified for European competition. The tributes to Jimmy were warm and heartfelt. Two of his former Morton colleagues, Tommy Orr and Billy Campbell, had also played with him for Scotland and knew him as well as anyone. For Billy Campbell, Jimmy was 'One of nature's gentlemen, an inspiration.' Tommy Orr commented, 'Jimmy carried his keen sense of sportsmanship off the field as well as on it.' The *Greenock Telegraph* tribute ended with the line 'He has a place in the heart of everyone who loves the game to which he gave so much.'

So just how good was Jimmy Cowan? His speciality was cross balls. He wasn't the biggest of goalkeepers – he stood about 5ft 11in, but he commanded his area with his imposing presence. Anything inside the six-yard area was his, even if it meant taking a teammate out to get the ball. And of course as he played in the days when forwards were allowed to put in heavy challenges on goalkeepers, and shoulder charges were de rigeur, so he had to be robust. He was a brilliant reaction 'keeper, and above all was as brave as they come. He was also a thinker, being one of the first goalkeepers to realise that his position was specialised. This led to coaching from Harry Rennie, who was a great theorist of the game, and ahead of his time as regards the coaching of goalkeepers.

Jimmy's 25 caps were all won when playing for a small provincial club, who more often than not were battling relegation. Indeed, several of his caps were won when Morton were in Scotland's old 'B' Division. He won his caps when internationals by and large consisted of Home Internationals, and the odd friendly, so it is safe to say that his cap total would be the equivalent of 60 or 70 in modern terms. A shy, modest man off the field, Jimmy would come alive on match days, no doubt emboldened by his teammates' cry of 'Have no fear, here comes Cowan'.

For a true summation of Jimmy's worth, who better to comment than the people who played with and against him? Lawrie Reilly said:

> *The greatest keeper I ever played with, no doubt. When I was asked to name my greatest Scotland side, then Jimmy Cowan was my choice. As*

Jimmy Cowan takes time out from training at Largs in 1952.

*far as I'm concerned it was Jimmy Cowan that beat England that day
[1949] with his first-half performance. If it hadn't been for Jimmy we
wouldn't have needed to have come out for the second half. The game
would have been all over. He gave us the encouragement to come out in
the second half and play them off the park.*

Eddie Turnbull of Hibernian made his Scotland debut in the same match as
Jimmy against Belgium at Hampden, and has fond memories of him, despite the
fact that his was one of the penalties Jimmy saved on his debut.

*Jimmy was a top class goalkeeper and a top class man. He was as brave
as they come, and he was the first to really think about the scientific
aspect of goalkeeping such as getting his angles right. I would rank him
as Scotland's best ever along with Jerry Dawson.*

Here are some facts about Jimmy's Scotland career. From his first cap against
Belgium in April 1948 to his last against Sweden in Scotland in May 1952,
Scotland played 27 international matches and Jimmy was between the posts in 25,
including 18 in succession. Scotland lost only seven of the matches he played in
and he lost an average of just over one goal per match, a pretty impressive statistic
given the number of goals scored per match in those days. Only three times in his
25 internationals did Jimmy let in more than two goals in a match, and in one of
those Scotland played much of the game with 10 men. His record compares
favourably with many of his successors. For example, Andy Goram, who is
generally rated as Scotland's finest modern-day goalie, conceded 34 goals in 43
matches in an era when defences were more tactically aware. Jimmy's caps total
of 25 was phenomenal 50 years ago, and at one stage he was the fifth most capped
Scotland player of all time behind such greats as Young, Morton, Walker and
Steel.

His talismanic presence undoubtedly helped Morton win many games they
would otherwise have lost, and but for injuries he would surely have stayed at the
top for longer and won many more caps. If anything his reputation has grown over

the years, and although he played his last match almost 50 years ago, Jimmy is still regularly touted as Scotland's greatest-ever goalkeeper.

The famous sports journalist Hugh McIlvany recently named Jimmy as his greatest-ever Scotland goalkeeper. When Jimmy's death was announced, the esteemed sports writer Hugh Taylor wrote that Jimmy's death had saddened the football world. Referring to Jimmy as 'The Prince of Goalkeepers' he wrote:

> *Jimmy Cowan's display at Wembley in 1949 was an epic of heroism and skill. Jimmy played few bad games, he could be acrobatic and daring, but his greatest asset was his reliability. He deserves his place in football's hall of fame.*

What better way than to remember Jimmy?

Morton playing statistics: (League, League Cup, Scottish Cup)

Season	Appearances
1946–47	1
1947–48	25
1948–49	25
1949–50	34
1950–51	36
1951–52	38
1952–53	32

Chapter 4

Allan McGraw
Mr Morton

It has become customary to use the words Allan McGraw and Morton in the same breath, but surely not as often as the words Allan McGraw and courage. For Allan McGraw the man is the very definition of courage. Allan's health problems over the past 30 years have been well documented. He played in an age when footballers were victims of some dubious methods of treating injuries. Often they were given running repairs, and took to the field when they shouldn't have. McGraw himself was given a painkilling jab on the eve of matches on innumerable occasions. As a result, Allan has endured countless operations on his knees, and is now unable to walk unaided. If he is bitter, it doesn't show. Allan still displays the same dignity, courtesy and forbearance that characterised his career as player, coach, manager and all-round footballing guru. As he says himself: 'Some people called me brave, but I would say I was stupid.'

An over-simplification perhaps, but it was Allan's willingness to go in where it hurts that resulted in the injuries that in turn led to the injections that allowed him to play. Arthur Montford's assessment of Allan the player perhaps sums him up best:

In terms of Scottish football, Allan was one of the finest strikers of all time. I know that may sound over the top, but Allan's ability both inside and outside the penalty area was breathtaking. I know that two of Scotland's greatest-ever forwards, Bob McPhail and Jimmy McGrory, rated Allan very highly indeed. And what a brave player he was. I know that he was persuaded wrongly to have injections to allow him to play. But he was so keen, and sadly that enthusiasm led to his immobility in later years. I would rate him along with his contemporaries Joe McBride and Jimmy Millar, and in the modern day, McCoist and Larsson.

Allan McGraw was born in Govan in 1939. His earliest memories are of constantly playing football in the streets, and he remembers being taken to Ibrox to watch Rangers draw with the famous Russian side Moscow Dynamo.

The young McGraw played schools football, and for juvenile side Partick Avondale. It may come as a surprise to those who know Allan McGraw as a brave and prolific goalscorer, but he was in fact a defender in his early career. He signed for Renfrew Juniors in 1957, and played as a centre-half for three years. His switch to the forward line only happened during his National Service in the army. Allan soon made a name for himself in army football, and represented the British Army. Top senior clubs coveted his signature, and he had the chance to sign for both Spurs and Newcastle United, but he opted for lowly Morton, then languishing at the foot of the Scotland's lowest division. The reason was straightforward. 'My father died while I was in the army and my mother was on her own. Hal persuaded me to sign by offering to fly me home every weekend.'

The 'Hal' in question was the inimitable Haldane Y. Stewart. A legendary figure in Morton's history, Hal took over Morton in 1961 and became one of the first managing directors in British football. 'The greatest challenge in the world' was his description of Morton at the time as he set about transforming Scotland's worst senior club into one of the most exciting sides in the land. Allan McGraw would become an integral part of the team that would become known as 'Hal's Heroes.'

'Hal was very persuasive,' says Allan. 'He was a likeable conman, and he was ahead of his time. People laughed at some of his ideas, but I've always said that if Hal had been at one of the Old Firm at that time they would be the biggest club in Europe now.'

Allan scored on his debut against Queen of the South, and under the expert coaching of some seasoned professionals Morton were on a roll. Allan says 'I learned more from Doug Cowie and Bobby Evans than any manager or coach I ever worked with. They were also two of the best players I ever played with.'

Morton narrowly missed out on promotion two seasons in a row in 1961–62 and 1962–63. During these two seasons Allan scored a half century of goals in less than 60 matches. By the 1963–64 season Allan was the focal point of the most exciting side seen at Cappielow since the days of Cowan, Campbell and Orr. They won their first 23 League matches in a row, and by October had reached the League Cup Final, a tremendous achievement for a second division side. A penalty from Allan secured their place in the final, as Morton defeated Hibernian 1–0 in a semi-final replay at Ibrox in front of huge numbers of Morton supporters. Surprisingly, this was the first penalty Allan had ever taken:

> *We'd had a bit of a problem with penalties and we'd missed two or three in a row, so Hal told me to take the penalties from then on. But we didn't get any for a while until the semi against Hibs, and I'd forgotten all about it. But Jim Reilly told me to take it, and I was never a confident penalty taker anyway, so I asked around if anybody else wanted to take it, and nobody wanted it. When I went to take it, I looked and Ronnie Simpson was standing off the centre of his goal near the right-hand post, so I just stuck it in the big end. Years later I spoke to Ronnie Simpson and he admitted it was a deliberate ploy to fool the kicker into aiming for the wee end. But I just stuck it away in the corner – in the big end. I scored 21 penalties in a row, but I couldn't say I enjoyed taking penalties. I fluffed one in against Jim Cruickshank at Hearts, and that was the last penalty I ever took.*

As for the final itself, the bare statistics, a 5–0 victory for Rangers in front of a then record crowd of 106,000, do not tell the true story of the match. Allan says that Morton were confident going into the match and actually thought they could win it. After a goalless first half in which Morton could have scored twice, Morton collapsed somewhat in the second half. But they had given a great account of themselves, and the final score did not reflect the state of play.

Allan says:

I hit the bar twice, and should have scored one of them. But I blame Hal for the heavy defeat. At half-time Jim Kiernan, who was a great centre-half, was a bit worried about his pace, because he was against Jim Forrest who was fast. So Hal pulled back Jim Reilly and we lost the midfield. Morris Stevenson, who was a dribbler, was left to do it all himself.

The heavy defeat did not derail Morton's season and they went on to win the second division title with a record of played 36, drawn three, lost one. They scored 135 goals in the process, with Allan scoring 50. His total in all competitions for the season was a club record of 58, making him Britain's top goalscorer. Yet Allan plays down his goal-grabbing achievements:

Joe Caven made a lot of goals for me, and Bobby Adamson, Morris Stevenson, and Jimmy Wilson take a lot of credit as well. It was a team full of characters. Jim Reilly, Jimmy Mallan, Bobby Adamson, Jimmy Wilson. Great characters.

Allan played at a time when Scottish football was full of great characters, and he has no hesitation in naming his favourite players:

Jim Baxter was my favourite player, the best footballer I ever saw, but Dave Mackay would be the first name on my team sheet. He had everything – the heart of a lion, as hard as nails, but he could play a bit as well. A great player.

In the very same season that Allan was breaking scoring records, another young Scottish number 10 was at the peak of his goalscoring powers. Denis Law was crowned European Footballer of the Year in 1964, and the similarities with Allan were self-evident. Both were quick, brave, exciting to watch, and tremendous finishers. And they worked for the team. Allan rejects any 'poacher' accusations:

Sometimes I get upset at people when they say I was just a poacher. I was a hard worker. Sometimes when people say you're a poacher they think you're lazy. I don't think anyone can lay that accusation against me. I worked my socks off, because I enjoyed playing so much.

Morton consolidated their first division status the following season, but by then Allan had began to miss matches through injury, although he still managed 21 goals. He was barely able to train, was losing mobility in his knees, and was relying more and more on the injections to allow him to play. He is philosophical about his injuries and the steps taken to render him fit to play. Used too often cortisone can lead to the complete disintegration of tissue and joints, which is why Allan's legs are now a mass of plastic and metal.

In those days we didn't know the effects of cortisone. The thing was, if you took a cortisone injection you were then supposed to rest. But I would then go out and play. I should have been smarter though, because I used to go to hospital for the injections, and I never saw the same doctor twice. I should have queried that. It was only later that I found out that the maximum safe number of injections in a year was three. I took 25 in one season! But I was just so keen to play.

It was also a tribute to Allan that he was such an important player that such drastic measures to render him fit were taken. There is no suggestion that anyone at the club knew the dangers involved, and Allan admits he didn't need much persuading, but the scars are more than physical. In his time as manager Allan never knowingly allowed one of his players to take a painkilling injection.

Morton finished a respectable 10th in their first season back in the top league, and a particular highlight for Allan was a game at Cappielow against Kilmarnock

McGraw pictured in 1964.

in December 1964. 'I had just come back from injury and I scored four goals, and that's the year Kilmarnock won the league, and I would say that was probably my finest performance.' In fact, Allan had just returned to fitness after a cartilage operation, and he helped Morton inflict Killie's first league defeat of the season.

Rex of the *Sunday Mail*'s match report of 13 December 1964 proclaimed Allan as 'Mr Dynamite' and posed the question, 'If Dundee's Alan Gilzean is worth £72,500, one wonders what Greenock's Alan is worth... the freedom of every boat in the Greenock docks?' The match report also underlines the accuracy of Allan's assessment of his striking partner Joe Caven, as Caven was credited with making three of Allan's goals.

Allan again missed much of the following season, 1965–66, and Morton were relegated. They bounced straight back with another high-scoring team, and with Joe Mason replacing Allan as the side's prolific goalscorer, Allan agreed to a transfer to Hibs in 1966. It was a wrench to leave Cappielow, but on the face of it a good move for Allan. Hibs were a bigger club, and it gave Allan the opportunity to work with Bob Shankly, brother of the famous Bill.

> *Bob Shankly was the only completely honest manager I ever met, and he always defended his players. Hal had turned down offers from Chelsea, Wolves, and Newcastle over the years, and it was good business for Morton, but I felt that Hibs didn't see the best of me. They had signed an injured player.*

Nevertheless, he gained new admirers at Easter Road, and often disguised injuries so that he could play in matches. However, his injuries had resulted in Allan losing some of his sharpness and pace, and he actually reverted to wing-half for much of his time with Hibs. 'I enjoyed my time with Hibs, but in 1971 I joined Linfield. They were playing in European competition, and were looking for experience,' Allan recalls.

Allan stayed in Belfast for a few months before returning home, where he reverted to the junior ranks, playing and coaching with Johnstone Burgh. In 1972 he joined Pollok as coach and quit playing altogether. 'Most players don't know when to retire and play on past their best. I can understand that. Because your playing days are your best days. I was lucky in a way, I was forced to retire.'

While still in his mid-thirties, Allan had the first of many operations on his knees. He was told by the surgeon that he had the legs of a 70-year old and would never run again.

Any anxieties Allan had about what the future might hold were allayed in 1974 when he was asked by the then Morton manager, old teammate Erik Sorenson, to coach the reserves. Hal Stewart's bold experiment with Scotland's first foreign manager was to end in tears and the sack for Erik shortly afterwards, but his decision to bring Allan back to Cappielow must go down as the most inspired and fortuitous in Morton's history. Allan didn't waste any time in bringing an assembly line of promising youngsters to the club. By the time Benny Rooney took over as manager in 1976, Allan was able to supply him with the precocious talents of Neil Orr, John McNeil, Joe McLaughlin and Jim Tolmie. Before long, with the outrageous talents of Andy Ritchie, allied to the professionalism of the likes of Davie Hayes, Jim Holmes and George Anderson, Rooney had built the most exciting Morton team since Allan's League Cup Final side. The mention of Andy Ritchie brings out a mixture of emotions in Allan.

> *There's not many things that make me angry, but that's one of them. What a player, what a talent, what a waste. He could do things with the ball that even Maradona couldn't. He could have been a superstar. And that makes me angry. He wasted his talent, but that was Andy. And a great guy... the nicest guy you could possibly meet. But he just didn't want it enough. I remember one day Benny Rooney said 'We'll need to get the big man working more.' I said 'Benny, if Jock Stein cannae get Andy working, what chance have we got?'*

Allan rates that Morton side as one of the club's finest. 'They were a bunch of rogues and scoundrels. I'd have hated to have managed them, but they could play.'

Morton's glory days in the Premier League ended with relegation in 1983, and Benny Rooney was sacked. A succession of short-term appointments followed with varying success. Neil Orr, Joe McLaughlin and others who had come through the McGraw youth system were all transferred for large fees.

After one more season in the Premier League under Willie McLean, Morton

Allan McGraw in typical goalscoring action beating Tommy Gemmell to the ball to net against Celtic at a packed Cappielow in 1964. John Fallon is the Celtic goalkeeper.

were once again relegated having endured a disastrous season during which they won only four matches and conceded a century of goals. Willie McLean left the club, and Morton were looking for their sixth manager in two years. It shouldn't have been so difficult. He had been there all the time. In 1985, a quarter of a century after he first signed for the club, Allan McGraw at last became manager of his beloved Morton.

> *Chairman Hugh Currie approached me to take over as manager, and I pointed out the obvious to him in that I wasn't very mobile. Hugh told me that all he needed was my heart and brain. That was good enough for me. I appointed Jackie McNamara, a good player and coach, as my assistant, and set about restructuring the youth policy which had fallen by the wayside.*

In his first season, 1985–86, Allan stabilised the club and they finished mid-table, but his aim was Premier League football. 'It took me four years to get the youth policy established, so I had to sign some experienced players like Lex Richardson and Rowan Alexander to help us back into the Premier League.'

Arguably Allan's best signing was Rowan Alexander, signed for a song from Brentford at the start of season 1986–87. Rowan gave almost 10 years sterling service to the club, and his 23 League goals were a deciding factor in Morton winning the first division that season by just one point. Sadly, the club's return to the Premier League lasted only one season as they were relegated once again the following term, winning only three matches. Allan explains:

> *As was so often the case with Morton, we just fell short. The money wasn't there to buy the players we needed, and the kids weren't ready. But from that season on, I decided that a successful youth policy was the only way forward for Morton.*

The remainder of Allan's managerial career at Morton saw a virtual assembly line of young talent being nurtured and sold on. It is no exaggeration to say that

John Boyd   H Mallen   Ian Miller   Jim Reilly   Jim Roman   W R Strachan

Bobby Campbell   Morris Stevenson   Joe Caven   Allan McGraw   Jimmy Wilson

The Morton team in 1964. Allan McGraw is seated in the front row, second from right.

without Allan's gift for spotting, developing, and selling on young players Morton might well have gone out of business. As ever, Allan prefers to give others their share of the credit. The names Jake Anderson and John Kerr are frequently mentioned by Allan when tributes are paid to those responsible for one of the best youth policies ever seen at a Scottish club. In a few short years players like Derek McInnes, David Hopkin, Derek Collins, Alan Mahood, Brian Reid and Allan's own son, Mark, were sold to bigger clubs. The real achievement was how Allan and his assistant John McMaster also managed to keep Morton in the promotion hunt despite losing so many fine young players, all the time playing attacking, entertaining football. As Allan says, 'I've never set out to defend in my whole career. Football is an entertainment.' Some fans were unhappy about the sale of the club's best players, but Allan is unrepentant.

> *I have no right to stop any player bettering themselves. Football's the same as any job in that respect. And some players deserve success. Look at Joe McLaughlin. When he first came to Morton he was a big, raw lad who could only head a ball. That was all he had. But I've never seen a player work as hard to improve his game as Joe did. And he reaped the benefits.*

Unfortunately Morton could not continue to sell their best players and hope to return to the Premier League, and in fact, after an injury-hit season in 1993–94, they were relegated to the second division. Allan received funds and was able to finance the signing of two quality players from Finland, Marko Rajamaki and Janne Lindberg, and Morton bounced straight back in one season, as ever, as Champions. The 1995–96 season that followed was one of the most exciting ever seen at Cappielow. Most managers would have been happy to consolidate for a season, but not Allan. His natural eye for a striker had secured the signing of Warren Hawke to play alongside the emerging Derek Lilley, and with a midfield of Lindberg, Alan Mahood and Derek McInnes, Morton played tremendous football all season and pushed the more fancied Dunfermline and Dundee United all the way. Allan remembers:

> *Lindberg, Mahood, and McInnes was the best midfield ever at Cappielow. Unfortunately, Derek had been promised a move, and when Rangers came in, we couldn't stand in his way. I then lost Lindberg to injury, and we ended up with central defenders in midfield.*

Allan doesn't say so, but one gets the impression that if he had been given the money to sign a midfielder then Morton would not have missed out on the Championship by just three points. Certainly the timing of the McInnes move (with two-thirds of the season to go) and the failure to replace him was puzzling. As it was, Morton missed out on a play-off place on goal difference. Fate decreed that the last game of the season was against play-off rivals Dundee United. Morton had to win to finish second and gain a play-off place, but United only needed a draw. An incredible 14,000 crowd packed into Cappielow for a 2–2 draw, and Morton just missed out. Allan McGraw was at the peak of his managerial career. His position as Scotland's premier talent spotter was unchallenged, and he was routinely hailed as the 'nicest man in football.' Enter Hugh Scott. In 1997 Morton chairman and owner John Wilson sold the club to 'businessman' Hugh Scott. The rest is history.

When Scott took over, he told me that he wanted a younger fitter, manager, which I could understand. But he also told me he wanted me to groom a new manager. I never got that chance. He appointed Billy

Allan McGraw celebrates his 58 goals in 48 appearances with this staged photograph in season 1963–64.

Stark as manager, and made me 'Director of Football.' I've never understood what that means. Anyway I spent about three months just hanging around not doing very much. I wouldn't want any manager looking over their shoulder at me, so I resigned.

It was a sad and undeserved end to a wonderful career with Morton. If Allan is bitter or resentful over the way he was treated he doesn't show it. 'Bitterness is a wasted emotion. But it's a misconception that supporters get managers the sack. Chairmen get managers the sack.' Dignified as ever, that is Allan McGraw's last word on Hugh Scott.

In the years since he left Morton Allan has faced more adversity with the death of his beloved wife and more operations. He has dabbled in politics, serving as a local councillor, and has been honoured by his peers, and by the Variety Club of Great Britain. His position as Morton's greatest ambassador is unchallenged, and it was this accolade that allowed Allan to effortlessly bring together many disparate parties in the 'Save The 'Ton' campaign when Morton almost went out of business during the Hugh Scott regime. These days Allan is surprisingly mobile. The prognosis of a decade ago that he might have to consider amputation as his only release from the constant pain from his knees has thankfully not been borne out. He now has to rely on only one stick, still drives, plays golf with the aid of a buggy, and is kept very active by his grand-daughter. However, he is scheduled for yet another operation on his right knee sometime in 2005. 'A wee problem with my knee' is how Allan euphemistically refers to it.

By Allan's reckoning this will be his 31st operation on his knees. In one memorable article the author reckoned the state of Allan's knees would have given Barry Sheene nightmares. And Allan has had many other battles to fight. During a match at Cappielow in the mid-1990s he was taken ill and had a heart attack 10 days later that resulted in bypass surgery a year later. He has also had two unpublicised bouts of cancer that are now thankfully in remission. The man is most definitely a survivor. He retains his natural enthusiasm for the game, but worries about its future, and the future of clubs like Morton.

Allan McGraw receives the Bell's First Division Manager of the Month award from John Beaton of Bell's in October 1995.

The only way forward for a club like Morton is a successful youth policy. People wondered how a club like Morton could compete against the Old Firm when it came to signing youngsters. It was hard, but we were able to offer them first-team football much quicker and a chance to move on to a bigger club if they were successful.

One example of the above is Allan's own son, Mark, who learned his trade under Allan at Cappielow before moving on to Hibs in 1991. Unfortunately, Mark also fell victim to an injury that curtailed his promising career. Mention of his son Mark brings Allan to talk about the things he found hard to handle in football.

Freeing young players. I hated that. I wouldn't sleep for a week when I

Back at Cappielow. Allan McGraw returns to work after suffering a heart attack six weeks previously in January 1996.

had to give a boy a free transfer. I looked on it that I was killing their dream. I never got used to it. I always hated it. I also found it hard managing my own son. I actually asked Cloughie [Brian Clough] *for his advice as he had managed his own son at* [Nottingham] *Forest. Cloughie just told me to treat him like any other player. But it was hard.*

The precarious state of Scottish football worries him.

It always puzzles me how chairmen of football clubs are successful in business, but their business sense goes out the window when they take over a club. They let their heart rule their head. And managers have to take a share of responsibility as well. A lot of people say managers aren't responsible. If they want money for a player they'll take it at all costs, and I'm not saying that's wrong. But as a manager you have to use your business common sense as well. We would all take the money, without thinking about the club. But I think the club is more important than any individual. And managers have to take responsibility as well, not just the directors.

Allan should know what he is talking about. Under John Wilson's chairmanship in the 1990s Morton were one of the most financially viable clubs in Scotland, one of only two in the black, prior to the Hugh Scott takeover. 'I hope John Wilson gets his credit sometime, because he got a lot of stick. But he ran a well-run ship.'

Allan's role in the 'Save The 'Ton' campaign confirmed once and for all the affection that Morton Football Club inspires. 'When the supporters asked me to help, I went around a lot of business people, and there was a lot of help, and that's when you realise that Morton means a lot to people.' It was through Allan's contacts that Morton were saved in the short term, but Allan is also quick to praise the fans and people in the community who, although not being Morton fans, put their hands in their pockets or helped in many other ways. Because as Allan says: 'The club is part of the community. That's why it's great that there is a supporter from the Supporters' Trust on the board.'

Allan is genuinely delighted that Morton have bounced back from near extinction and are now doing so well both on and off the park. 'Douglas Rae [Morton chairman and owner] loves the club, and he's the right man for the job. He will never do Morton any harm.' Allan holds strong views on the modern game. He believes the wages being paid nowadays are 'obscene', but doesn't blame the players. 'The players are taking all the money out of the game now, but I don't blame them. I blame the chairmen for paying the huge salaries.'

He also believes that players should be more accountable. He thinks that they should involve themselves more with the community and put something back into the game, something he always encouraged when Morton manager.

Allan still attends matches occasionally, but football must look at itself if there is no place in it for a man like Allan McGraw. As a player, there was no one braver, and as a manager and coach there was no one better at spotting and developing young talent. The list of players who owe a debt of gratitude to Allan for starting them off on their careers is a very long one indeed. For Derek McInnes, Allan was the man who started it all for him.

Allan McGraw
finally says
goodbye to
Morton in 1997.

I signed on a YTS contract at 16. The Boss told me it wasn't down to age. If I was good enough I was old enough. And he was true to his word. I made my debut at 16. I had the utmost respect for him from day one, always felt I had his trust and confidence. He made you feel confident, impressed upon me that mistakes were all part of a learning curve. I have a lot to thank him for, and it's more than a coincidence that so many of his young players did so well in the game.

McGraw has real standing among older and more experienced pros. As Rowan Alexander explains:

I have nothing but total and undivided respect for the man. I will always be grateful for him bringing me back up from England and giving me a chance in Scottish football again. His expertise and knowledge played a big part in my success at Morton and I owe him a lot. His all round presence and stature as a man gains respect from everyone in the game. I remember his brief but sensible team talks, his all round knowledge, and his achievements as a player. I absolutely loved playing for him.

Morton Football Club are indeed fortunate that they have had the services of this unassuming, modest man. He truly is Mr Morton.

Morton playing statistics: (League, League Cup, Scottish Cup)

Season	Appearances	Goals
1961–62	16	14
1962–63	43	36
1963–64	48	58
1964–65	33	21
1965–66	36	11

Chapter 5

Joe Harper
Little Joe – A Goals
Bonanza

Morton fans, perhaps more than any others, love it when one of their own makes the grade for their club. For Joe Harper, born and bred in Greenock, playing for his home town team was the realisation of a dream. That he should do so at the tender age of 16 is all the more remarkable. If Aberdeen fans can lay claim to Joe Harper as the 'King of Pittodrie' then Morton fans can justifiably argue that they had a prior claim. Long before his goalscoring exploits for Aberdeen, the young Harper endeared himself to the Morton fans with his enthusiasm, bubbly personality, skill, and eye for goal. It is rare for a footballer to become a hero twice over, but Joe managed that feat at Aberdeen, and his time at Morton is fondly remembered both by himself and the Morton fans, for the special rapport between them. So much so, that in a recent poll Joe was voted the eighth greatest Morton player of all time, pretty impressive when one considers that it's 35 years since Joe played for the club. He may also be the only Scottish player to receive a tribute from that doyen of centre-forwards, Roy Race. The famous comic book centre-forward of Melchester Rovers penned his own special tribute to Joe during Joe's testimonial year at Aberdeen.

Joe Harper was born in Greenock in 1948 and he was brought up in the Belville Street area in the East End of the town less than 10 minutes walk from Cappielow. Joe was one of the ubiquitous 'street' footballers, spending most of his time playing football on the street with lamp posts for goals, and in doing so unwittingly honing his skills. Joe says:

> People ask now, 'Why don't we see kids playing football in the street now?' But in those days we were lucky to see one car in our street. Nowadays every street in Britain has tons of cars, so even if the kids wanted to, they couldn't play in the streets.

A young Joe gets his hands on some silverware at Belville Street School in 1960.

Even as a young boy Joe had the happy knack of scoring goals, and his name was often to be found in the local paper as his reputation grew. His early football career encompassed school, Boys Brigade and youth football, and it was as a pupil of Greenock Mount High School that Joe first played at Cappielow in several Schools Cup Finals. Joe received great encouragement and help from his schoolteachers, and actually excelled in other sports apart from football. He played cricket and rugby, but football was everything to him. While playing for Larkfield Boys Club aged 15, Joe was offered a trial for Junior side Irvine Meadow in a friendly match. Unknown to Joe the match had been arranged in order for a Rangers scout to watch Joe in action. Joe scored a hat-trick.

After the match this guy came up to me, and I still didn't know who he was and told me that he was very impressed but thought I was still a bit too small, although they would keep an eye on me. It was only when I told my dad afterwards that I found out that he was a Rangers scout. My dad had known all along but hadn't let on.

But Rangers were not the only club interested. 'A few days later I was sitting in the house and there was a knock at the door. My dad answered it and it was Hal Stewart.' Hal Stewart was then in the early stages of his golden period as managing director of Morton. The man who had very little experience in football had come to Cappielow in 1961 and transformed Morton from the worst side in the Scottish leagues to an emerging, exciting, resurgent club, who were about to take Scottish football by storm. He was a super salesman who, that night in Joe's house, won over the Harper family.

Hal swept into the house and straight away asked me if I'd like to sign for Morton. I told him that I would have to speak to my dad and grandad before I could give him a decision. So Hal went away and my dad and grandad had a wee chat. My dad, who was obviously very impressed by Hal, said, 'If you're going to make it in football we think that you're better going to Morton. You'll have a better chance there than with a big

**A youthful
Joe Harper
in training.**

Joe Harper scores the winner against Dundee United in the Scottish Cup Quarter final of 1969.

*club like Rangers where you could be a small fish in a big pond.' That
was good enough for me; in fact I was a bit of a Morton fan anyway. Just
a couple of weeks previously I had been caught by the railway police
cutting over the railway line to get into Cappielow.*

So Joe signed for Morton in 1963 just as the club were entering one of the most
exciting and memorable seasons in their history. Their record-breaking side ran
away with the second division and reached the League Cup Final in October 1963
where they faced Rangers. As a member of the ground staff, Joe experienced all
the menial tasks associated with that role such as getting the training gear ready
and brushing the terracing. 'John Ellis was the stadium manager, and he would
get us to brush the terraces with stories of him finding 50 quid one day. I think
the most we ever found was a tanner.'

But Joe was also immediately involved in training with the first-team squad. It
all kicked off for Joe in May 1964 when Morton were at Firhill against Partick
Thistle in the short-lived Summer Cup. Joe and two of his ground staff pals
travelled up on the train to watch the match.

*We went for something to eat in Glasgow and then walked to Firhill. It
must have been about twenty past two when we arrived to be greeted by
a doorman who stopped us from getting into the ground despite our
protestations that we were Morton players. I even showed him my Morton
tie but unimpressed he said to me, 'Away ye go son, if you're lucky
somebody will gie ye a punt over.' But just at that moment Hal Stewart
came out, pulled me aside, and asked me if I'd had anything to eat. As
soon as he said that I knew something was about to happen.*

Unbeknown to Joe one of the Morton players had taken unwell, and the call had
gone out for Joe Harper. 'Hal said to me, "Get changed, you're playing". By this
time it was about twenty five to three which actually worked out in my favour
because I had no time to get nervous.'

Aged 16, Joe made his first-team debut against a very experienced Thistle side that included George Niven, Harold Davis and Donnie McKinnon, and scored the only goal of the match. '*Bonanza* was very popular on the television at that time, and one of the characters was 'Little Joe', so of course the Sunday papers were full of headlines the next day like 'Little Joe shoots down Thistle.'

It was a memorable introduction to first-team football for Joe, who at that stage only stood about 5ft 5in tall, so the 'Little Joe' comparisons were apt. At this stage of his career Joe was a right winger with a natural inclination to come inside and look for scoring opportunities. But with players such as Allan McGraw, Joe Caven and Carl Bertleson at the club, as well as his small stature, Joe rarely got a chance in the centre-forward position. At the end of Joe's first season at the club Morton had won promotion back to the first division with their record-breaking side, and it was a tremendously exciting time to be at the club. Hal Stewart's next and possibly greatest innovation was the Scandinavian invasion. Joe cites the influx of Danish players as a major factor in his development as a player.

> *After training in the mornings the Danish players would stay back and practice, probably out of boredom, because in Greenock in the sixties there wasn't much else to do! But I would stay back with them. They were the first players I saw that would do this. It was great for me because Erik Sorensen as a goalkeeper was so proud that he hated the ball hitting the back of the net, whereas I loved the ball hitting the net. So we used to go out on the park, and guys like Preben Arentoft, Carl Bertlesen and Fleming Neilson would put crosses in and I'd head them, try overhead kicks, scissor kicks, everything. And it was all about hitting the target, hitting the net, and it was great education for me. Subconsciously I was learning all the time.*

It is impossible to talk about Morton in the 1960s without mentioning the 'Danish Invasion.' Danish club football in those days was largely amateur, and after a Morton tour there in 1963 Hal Stewart realised that there was a golden opportunity to benefit Morton. From 1964 Hal brought over to Greenock a number of top-class players, the first of whom, goalkeeper Erik Sorensen, made a lasting impact. He was dubbed 'The Man in Black' on his debut, due to his habit of playing in an all black strip, and immediately impressed with his agility, ability, and all-round competence. Others followed in Erik's wake. Class players such as Kai Johansen and Jorn Sorensen were signed, and the threesome were then all moved on to Rangers for substantial fees. And so followed a familiar pattern. In one league match Morton played six Danes, and this was long before the influx of foreign players into the Scottish game in the 1980s and 1990s. But these players differed wildly from some of the mercenaries that have so blighted Scottish football in recent seasons. They were tremendously gifted, dedicated, professional players. The arrangement suited both parties. The players would receive good remuneration for their efforts, and were allowed to move on to bigger clubs if they were good enough. And for their initial outlay, Morton would benefit from the transfer fee. And as Joe says, he benefited as a professional by training and playing with these players. Preben Arentoft and Fleming Nielson were two excellent signings for Morton. Nielson had played in the Italian League, and 'Tofty' was transferred to Newcastle, winning a Fairs Cup winners' medal.

Joe continued to serve his apprenticeship in the first team, and season 1965–66 saw Joe eager to win a permanent first-team place, but with Morton struggling in the league and eventually being relegated, opportunities were few. Joe still managed to score six goals in 12 league matches, however, but he easily eclipsed that the following season as he at last gained the regular first-team spot he craved. Morton won the second division at a canter with another high-scoring side. Joe formed a tremendous partnership with Joe Mason, who had been with Kilmarnock when they won the first division title in 1965. Joe Mason was a tremendously exciting player to watch, brave and acrobatic. He was a personality player who became a huge favourite at Cappielow. His 43 goals in season 1966–67 helped 'Ton fans to get over the loss of Allan McGraw to Hibs, and in his first 64 games for Morton, Mason scored an incredible 68 goals. Joe Harper himself scored 29 goals in 30 league matches that season. At this stage he was still nominally a right winger but rarely stayed on the touchline, preferring to get in the box as much as possible.

Morton fans took to Joe immediately. Because he was a local boy they could

Joe Harper celebrates his hat-trick against Partick Thistle in 1968. Billy Ritchie is the Jags goalkeeper.

identify with him, and his boundless enthusiasm and joy at scoring goals endeared him to the fans.

Joe's goals had attracted the attention of bigger clubs, but when he did move it was to Yorkshire and second division Huddersfield in February 1967 for £35,000:

I didn't even know where Huddersfield was and I was happy at Morton and didn't really want to move. But the way they sold it to me was that Denis Law had started at Huddersfield, and I was going to be the new Denis Law.

Morton had virtually won the second division when Joe was transferred, and were gearing themselves up for the next season, so the timing of the transfer was puzzling, but summed up the philosophy at Cappielow – everyone was for sale at the right price.

Joe endured a miserable time in Yorkshire although he did get the chance to play with a young Frank Worthington. Not long after he joined Huddersfield Joe was named in a Scotland tour party for the grandly named World Tour. The pool consisted of Scotland fringe players or players for the future and included, among others, Willie Morgan and a certain Alex Ferguson, then of Dunfermline. It was a month-long tour, taking in Israel, Australia, New Zealand and Canada. The Scots played a number of matches against representative sides of the respective countries. They weren't recognised as full internationals, but nevertheless in Joe's two matches he scored three in one and five in the other. If only Hal Stewart had held on to Joe for a bit longer he could have got more for him!

Joe had kept in touch with Hal Stewart while at Huddersfield and within 18 months he was back at Cappielow for half the original transfer fee. Joe soon had the Morton fans chanting his name again. He was playing more often in his favoured position of centre-forward, and the goals began to flow again. Joe's return to Cappielow came at an exciting time for the club. Their first season back in the top division had ended in a top-six finish and qualification for Europe in the old Fairs Cities Cup. Not for Morton fans though the heady delights of a tie against Real Madrid or Inter Milan. Morton were drawn against Chelsea, who were actually a pretty glamorous side with talented players like Charlie Cooke and Peter Osgood. Unfortunately, Morton's first and to date only European venture was to end in a 9–3 aggregate defeat, but not before they had given the London glamour boys a few frights in the second leg at Cappielow. The first leg at Stamford Bridge had ended in a 5–0 thrashing despite Morton giving a good account of themselves in the first half. The return leg saw the Cappielow faithful turn out in large numbers to see a top-class English outfit in the flesh, hoping that Morton wouldn't be thrashed again. What they got was a classic rollercoaster cup tie in the best Cappielow tradition. Chelsea scored early to further deflate the 'Ton fans, but Morton, realising they had only pride to play for, threw caution to the wind, and launched wave upon wave of attacks. Amazingly, Morton found themselves 3–1 up after 27 minutes, and had two decent penalty claims turned down as Chelsea defended desperately. However, any hopes of a miraculous comeback were dashed as Chelsea regrouped to draw level at 3–3 at half-time. The second half saw Morton still chasing the game, but it was Chelsea who triumphed 4–3 with a goal seven minutes from the end. It had been a magnificent effort by Morton, and who would have thought 36 years later they would still be waiting for a second attempt at European football?

Joe was just happy to be back with Morton after his Huddersfield nightmare, and settled very quickly back into his groove. After playing in the Chelsea double header, Joe scored a tremendous hat-trick against Partick Thistle in October 1968. Morton were 3–1 down and Joe scored with two headers in the last 10 minutes. Photographs of the time captured Joe's joy at doing the thing he did best. Joe scored another hat-trick later that season against Hibs in a memorable match at Cappielow with 'Ton winning 4–3. Joe scored the winner with a free-kick which he swerved around the defensive wall. One week previously he had scored the winner in the Scottish Cup quarter-final at Tannadice to earn 'Ton a crack at Celtic in the semi. It was a purple patch for Joe, and with Joe Mason now playing in a deeper role, Joe found himself with several different striking partners. Probably the most effective was Dane Per Bartram, who figured prominently in one of Joe and Morton's most memorable performances. In April 1969, three days after Celtic had comprehensively beaten Rangers 4–0 in the Scottish Cup Final,

Morton travelled to Parkhead for a seemingly meaningless end-of-season league match. Celtic had also won the League and League Cup that year and there was a party atmosphere as they paraded the silverware before their adoring fans. Morton were just there to make up the numbers, weren't they? Joe says he remembers being a bit annoyed at having to applaud Celtic onto the park and then stand around as the Celtic players milked the applause from the huge crowd.

> *Hal Stewart said to us before the match that he wanted us to line up and applaud the Celtic players on to the field. I remember saying 'That'll be ******* right', but Hal said 'no, you'll do it.' Well we did but we then stuffed them 4–2.*

Indeed they did. In a memorable Morton performance 'Batman and Robin' as the duo were briefly christened, destroyed Celtic. Per Bartram scored a hat-trick in 10 first-half minutes and Joe scored the other to silence the huge Parkhead crowd. It was the type of performance that Morton would periodically muster against both halves of the Old Firm. Joe himself scored Morton's goal in a 1–1 draw at Cappielow earlier that season, but unfortunately they couldn't cause a shock in that season's Scottish Cup semi-final when Celtic won 4–1 after Willie Allan had put Morton ahead in the second minute. It was an exciting but ultimately disappointing time for Morton fans with regular trips to Hampden for semi-finals, always destined to end in defeat. Joe has nothing but fond memories of his early career.

> *I think I was born with a gift, but I'd play football anywhere with any type of ball. From organised football to my mum's hall with a tennis ball I was constantly playing, constantly practising and constantly learning. I came into football in a golden age. I was playing for what I considered to be a big club, and there was always a happy dressing room. When we reached the League Cup Final in '63 I travelled up with the team, and I actually thought we could win! There were some terrific players and characters at Cappielow. Joe Mason was a typical Ayrshire guy. Joe and Hughie Strachan were always winding the guys up, and Allan McGraw was a*

hero to everyone. Then the Danes came. That added a touch of class. Guys like Preben Arentoft, Erik Sorensen, Jorn Sorensen, Johnny Boyd were great pros, and Eric Smith was a good coach. Hal Stewart wasn't a manager as such. You never saw him in a track suit, he was always dapper, impeccably dressed. Hal was so far ahead of his time. When he was with the Co-op he launched Rangers and Celtic cigarettes, and he was always wheeling and dealing. Hal was a breath of fresh air. There was never a dull moment, he was always smiling, he was always funny, he was a good businessman, and he was a good man manager. With me being a local boy he was always hearing stories about me which were a lot of rubbish, and he told me that he soon learned to ignore them. I remember when we signed Per Bartram Hal gave him a big write-up in the papers, that he'd scored six goals in his last game. What he didn't say was that it had been a seven-a-side kick about! We never had a manager as such, just top-class coaches like Eric Smith, Bobby Howitt and Doug Cowie. When I look back on my time at Morton I think it was possibly the happiest of my career. Yet if I'd been a bit older, 23 or 24, I would prob-ably have been disappointed, because they always threatened to achieve more but it never quite happened. But I learned so much there, and I loved every minute of it. Look at the players I played with as a boy – Bobby Evans, Doug Cowie… Scotland legends. Allan, (McGraw) the Danes. Joe Caven, who was an underrated player, was a great help to me, and set me up for my first goal. It was all a great adventure for me, a great apprenticeship. I could walk to the park in 10 minutes, I was there all the time, football was my life. I played with some wonderful players; Allan McGraw, Morris Stevenson, Johnny Boyd. I used to play five-a-sides at the back of the car park with the likes of Doug Cowie, and I just loved that.

Allan McGraw saw first-hand the precocious talents of the young Harper at Morton and says:

He started out as a winger with Morton, but they only played him there to protect him. You could tell from an early age that he was going to be a striker, and what he great striker he was. He had two great feet and he certainly knew where the goal was. You could always rely on Joe to get you goals, and I always felt he should have won more caps.

Season 1969–70 was a watershed for Joe. He started the season in tremendous form for Morton with five goals in the League Cup as Morton reached the quarter-finals only to be knocked out after a replay. Little did he

Joe works on his technique at Cappielow in 1969.

know then that he would play in a cup final come the end of the season. Morton started the League season brilliantly, and after six matches were second top, with Joe scoring four goals. His form also earned him a League Cap against the League of Ireland along with Morton teammate Gerry Sweeney in December 1969. However, by then he was an Aberdeen player, having signed for the Dons in September for £40,000. It was the beginning of a two-way love affair between Joe and the Aberdeen fans. They immediately took him to their hearts when he scored with a penalty on his home debut. His first season at Aberdeen climaxed with a penalty as well, seven months later in the Scottish Cup Final against Celtic. This goal was as good an example as any of the famous Harper coolness. Aberdeen were awarded an early first-half penalty for hand ball, and Celtic protested long and hard. There was an incredibly long delay as the referee fought to restore order, and Joe killed the time by playing keepie-up with the ball. Eventually the coolest man inside Hampden tucked the ball away, and Aberdeen never looked back, gaining a famous victory. Joe had won silverware in his first season at Aberdeen and the next three seasons saw him become a hero with his goalscoring exploits.

Aberdeen fans were stunned therefore when he was transferred to Everton in 1972 for £180,000. 'It was similar to my move to Huddersfield. I didn't really want to go, but I was told that Aberdeen couldn't turn that kind of money down as it secured their financial future.'

So Joe tried his luck in England once more, but he had joined a club which was on a downward spiral, and things didn't work out too well, although he still managed a decent return of goals. By 1974 Eddie Turnbull was the manager at Hibs and he brought Joe home for a fee of £120,000. It's true to say that Joe has been immensely popular wherever he has played, with the obvious exception of Hibs. For one reason or another the Hibs fans just didn't take to him despite a healthy scoring rate and his usual unbridled enthusiasm. One theory was that soon after Joe signed the great Hibs side of that period began to break up, with immensely popular players such as Jim O'Rourke, Alan Gordon and John Brownlie being sold. Rightly or wrongly the Hibs fans interpreted these transfers as funding Joe's move. Consequently, he was never popular despite scoring goals for the club. He also scored a hat-trick in the 1974 League Cup Final and still ended up on the losing side. Joe returned to Aberdeen in 1976 and consolidated the legendary status that he still holds today. He completed a clean sweep of medals with League Cup and Championship winners' medals. Unfortunately, a cruciate injury finished Joe's career at the age of 32. He had a brief spell at Peterhead as player-coach, and settled in Aberdeen for many years before returning home to Greenock to run a pub. He is now back living in Aberdeen and works at the club as a match-day host. He was officially designated an 'Aberdeen Legend' in 2000, joining such Dons luminaries as Willie Miller, Alex McLeish and Bobby Clark.

Eddie Turnbull was the man who signed Joe for Aberdeen and he rated Joe highly enough to sign him again when he became manager of Hibernian.

> *Joe was a little gem, a born goalscorer. And I think centre-forwards are born, not made, and Joe was a born goalscorer. He was so cool in the box and he was a great guy to have in the dressing room. He was two footed and a good footballer who could bring others into the game. And when you were under the cosh Joe would pop up with a goal and relieve the pressure.*

For Joe's part he rates Turnbull as the best coach and manager he ever worked with. A hard taskmaster, Eddie was also not without humour as Joe remembers:

> *I remember asking Eddie Turnbull what the difference between technique and skill was. Eddie said, 'Technique is when the ball comes to you, you take it on your chest, onto your knee, onto your foot, then turn on a tanner and whip it into the net.' I said, 'okay, what's skill?' Eddie growled at me, 'Skill is daeing all that wi' John Greig up your arse!'*

Mention of John Greig brings Joe around to talking about opponents, and he says he enjoyed playing against the so-called hard men like John Greig, and also tall centre-halves like Billy McNeil. 'You knew where you were with these guys. Big Greig would always try to kick you but he could play a bit as well.'

As a player Joe's admiration for Billy Bremner knew no bounds and he rates Bremner as his favourite Scotland player and the best captain he ever played with. One thing, however, does irk Joe slightly about his career, and that is the fact that he only won four full caps, and two of them were as a substitute. However, as he says:

> I only played two full matches and scored two goals, so that's not a bad average, and although I only played 13 minutes as a sub in the World Cup, I still realised an ambition by doing so.

There is no doubt that when Joe was at his peak with Aberdeen he should have won more caps. It cannot be denied that Scotland were well off for strikers, but perhaps if he had been playing for one of the Old Firm his caps total would have been greater. So what were Joe's attributes as a player? He bridles at the suggestion that he was just a 'poacher.'

> Any good striker will always be called a poacher. Ally McCoist will always be known as a poacher, but there was more to his game, and it was the same with me. As I say, I think I was born with a gift, but all the practice I put in as a kid with any type of ball, from a tennis ball in my mother's hall to a paper ball when I was in hospital as a teenager paid dividends. I prided myself on my first touch, otherwise I wouldn't have scored as many goals. I had two good feet, I could bring others into the play, and my timing was good in the air. When I was young I worked constantly on my weaker left foot, so much so that it ended up better than my right. A lot of times it was just about hitting the target, but I scored a fair amount from outside the box, volleys, half volleys and the like. I remember watching a video of Pelé in training, and the work he put in practising everything from heading to volleying, overhead kicks, the lot. Then the video showed him in action, and he was putting all this into

practice in a match situation, and I thought back to those afternoons I spent in training with the Danes, and realised that it had all been beneficial.

A big influence on Joe was Gerd Muller, and the similarities are obvious. Both were small, stocky, chunky even, not exactly the athletic-looking type, but give them a ball at their feet and they were deadly. Possibly it was their build and small stature which gave them their low centre of gravity that enabled them to turn and swivel in the box, and find the net in an instant, just like Muller's goal in the 1974 World Cup Final against Holland, as Joe says himself: 'a typical Joe Harper type of goal.' After all, as Joe says, 'If you're going to compare yourself with someone, it might as well be the best.'

And as Roy Race might say 'Joe, you were one of the best.'

Morton playing statistics: (League, League Cup, Scottish Cup)

Season	Appearances	Goals
1964–65	3	1
1965–66	17	7
1966–67	41	30
1968–69	40 +1 sub	27
1969–70	15	9

Chapter 6

Jim Holmes Homer – The Perfect Professional

Morton fans know a thing or two, you know. Just ask Andy Ritchie, for many the greatest Morton player of all time. At the end of the 1978–79 season, big Andy had just been voted the Scottish Football Writers' Player of the Year for that season. He had taken the Premier League by storm with his extravagant skills and spectacular goals, and there could be no other choice for the honour. But who did the Morton fans vote for the club player of the year? Not Andy, who had scored over 30 goals that season, but a quiet, unassuming left-back, Jim Holmes, who three seasons previously had been given a free transfer by Partick Thistle. And really, not even Andy could begrudge Jim the honour, for as brilliant as Andy Ritchie was that season, Jim in his own quiet way was every bit as important a player to Morton. 'Homer' served Morton for 12 seasons, several of them as skipper, and was a model of professionalism and consistency. In a recent poll Jim was voted the fifth-greatest Morton player ever. International recognition unaccountably eluded him, but he gained the respect of everyone in the game. Whenever there are arguments over the best-ever uncapped Scottish players, then Jim's name is high on the list. Allan McGraw was at Cappielow for much of Jim's career, and he says:

Jim Holmes –
Viva Zapata!

Without doubt Jim was the best left-back Morton have ever had. He was the perfect professional. He had a great attitude, he was a great trainer, and was so consistent, not just game to game, but year by year. It's a complete mystery to me why he was never capped.

Jim Holmes was born in 1954 in Hamilton and brought up in nearby Bellshill, and his earliest memories are of playing football constantly, anywhere there was a game; whether it was a street kick-about or a more organised affair, Jim was there. He came from a football background, his grandfather having played for Cowdenbeath. Jim joined Muirkirk in the Ayrshire Junior Leagues in 1971, and was signed by Partick Thistle manager Davie McParland in 1974. At this stage Jim was a right-back and skippered Thistle Reserves to the Reserve League Cup. First-team opportunities were few with John Hansen, brother of Alan, at right-back, but Jim seemed to be progressing nicely. By 1976 Bertie Auld had taken over as Thistle manager, and Jim was surprisingly freed without playing a first-team match.

Perhaps for the notoriously defensively-minded Bertie, Jim was just a bit too adventurous going forward, but Thistle's loss was Morton's gain. Benny Rooney had just retired as a player at Thistle to take over as Morton boss in the summer of 1976, and when he heard that Jim was available, he made him one of his first signings.

I had played with Jim at Partick Thistle and I knew all about his qualities. When I took over at Cappielow, Jim was one of my first signings. He was just a good all round footballer, and a good athlete, very fit. He was very rarely injured because of his level of fitness. As he gained experience he just got better and better, and he became one of the best full-backs in the country. It goes without saying he should have been capped, and I was also surprised that he didn't move on to a bigger club, but I had no concrete offers for him. Not that I was complaining. Jim was a tremendous professional.

Jim made his Morton debut in a League Cup sectional match in midfield, and as Benny Rooney settled into the job he was experimenting with different players in different positions. Homer managed two goals from midfield in six League Cup matches, including a 25-yard rocket after a memorable solo run, but it soon became apparent that Morton were sorely in need of a left-back. At that stage skipper Davie Hayes was so firmly established as Morton's right-back and all-round cult hero, that Carlos Alberto and Danny McGrain would have been happy to play left-back, so Homer had no qualms about switching flanks. In the event, Jim settled immediately into his new position, quickly becoming a fans' favourite with his skilful and thoughtful play, and was an ever-present in his first season.

In October 1976 Benny Rooney sealed the bargain of the century when he

Holmes tackles the great Davie Cooper, of Glasgow Rangers.

somehow prised Andy Ritchie from Celtic, and then he set about moulding his Morton side around Andy's outrageous talents. In a memorable 1977 New Year's Day match at Cappielow Morton gave eventual champions St Mirren a fright before eventually succumbing to Alex Ferguson's exciting young side. Morton were 2–0 up after 10 minutes before goalkeeper Liddell was sent off. Morton used two replacements in goal, and eventually lost 6–3 in an incredible match. A sense of injustice was felt at Cappielow, but revenge was gained at the end of the season when Saints visited Cappielow for the final derby of that season. The Morton players lined up and applauded the new First Division Champions onto the field,

Another perfectly-timed Holmes intervention in a 1-1 draw with Kilmarnock at Rugby Park on 8 February 1986.

then thumped them 3–0. This victory came in the middle of a marvellous unbeaten run in the last third of season 1976–77. 'Ton remained unbeaten in the last 16 matches of that season and eventually finished fourth. Rooney's target was Premier Division football, and the more astute observers felt they were the side to watch in season 1977–78, despite the more fancied Dundee and Hearts being favourites for promotion. But 'Ton hit the ground running, resuming their excellent form of the last third of the previous season. With a young Mark McGhee up front scoring goals for fun, Morton continued their long unbeaten run. They were top of the first division from the off, and by the time of their first League defeat in October 1977, their unbeaten run stood at 27 games with 22 wins and five draws. Mark McGhee was one young player who benefited from Homer on and off the park:

> *Well, he was just Mr Consistency. Jim was an excellent footballing defender and a great team player. Always talking, always encouraging. I can hear him now actually as I'm talking about him. He was a great influence in the team, always ready to talk to you after a match on a one-to-one basis. Tremendous professional.*

With a sticky patch of form coinciding with the transfer of McGhee to Newcastle in Christmas 1977, the experts began to write Morton off. But they gave notice of things to come when they came back from 2–0 down in a Scottish Cup tie at Aberdeen with two goals in the last 10 minutes to take Aberdeen to a replay. It wouldn't be the last time that Morton would surprise the Dons, and they were unfortunate to lose the replay at Cappielow. With the outstanding Ritchie now feeding new arrival Bobby Russell, and Homer on the left side of Morton's finest-ever back four of Hayes, Anderson, Orr, and Holmes, Morton prevailed.

Promotion and the Championship were sealed on a memorable April night at Cappielow, with a 3–1 victory over Airdrie. As brilliant as Ritchie and Holmes were in that memorable promotion-winning season, it was the two 'old hands', Skipper Hayes and centre-half George Anderson, who did more than most to help 'Ton into the top league. The term 'old hand' does the two players a disservice, as they were, in fact, only in their mid-twenties, but both had made their debuts at

16 at the beginning of the decade, and they seemed to have been at Cappielow forever. In a 14-year career with Morton 'Hannibal' only scored three goals in 467 appearances, but two of them came in the promotion-winning season. One of them was in the match against Airdrie, and helped set 'Ton up for eventual victory, promotion, and the championship. George Anderson was a hard-as-nails centre-half, an Under-23 cap who had gone to South America on a tour with Tommy Docherty's Scotland aged only 18. Anderson once sent Malcolm MacDonald, the famously opinionated Newcastle centre-forward, scurrying back over the border complaining that 'Morton were the dirtiest team he had ever played against' after a particularly bruising encounter with Anderson in a so-called friendly. Anderson, that season's player of the year, scored nine league goals in the promotion-winning season, a tremendous total for a defender, and particularly significant given that Morton eventually won the title on goal difference.

Both Hayes and Anderson seemed to have made it their life's work to get Morton up to the Premier League. Anderson hailed from Port Glasgow, and another local boy, Neil Orr from Gourock, completed the back four. Neil, the son of Morton legend Tommy Orr, was only 19 when Morton clinched the league, but had been a regular for almost three seasons. Coming into the side at 17, Orr was a raw, lanky boy just like his father, but Anderson nursed him through his formative years, allowing him to make his mistakes and learn by them. By 1979, Neil was a regular for Scotland Under-21s, and seemed sure to follow his father into the full Scottish side. Jim recalls:

> *I played with a lot of terrific players at Cappielow, and that early side that won the first division had more than a few. Davie Hayes and George Anderson were Morton through and through, and there were young guys like Charlie Brown and John McNeil who probably never totally fulfilled their true potential, and big 'Goldie' (John Goldthorpe) up front was a great foil for big Andy.*

'Big Andy' was of course, the one and only Andy Ritchie, the most talented footballer ever to grace the blue and white hoops. He wasn't the hardest working of players but as Jim says: 'Andy was the man who put steak on our table,' meaning of course that he was a match-winner. 'The rest of the players were willing to do the hard work for the big man because one flash of his genius could guarantee a win bonus.'

So Homer had a second stab at the Premier League. He was now playing under a manager who encouraged open, exciting, attacking football. Jim and his full-back partner 'Hannibal' Hayes found their attacking instincts given full reign, and spent as much of the game in their opponents' half as they did defending their own. 'Most teams played 4–3–3 in those days with two strikers and a winger. If it was a left winger, Hannibal would mark him, and I would have the whole left side to myself, and vice versa.'

A Division One Player of the Year Award went to Holmes in 1987.

Morton began their debut season in the Premier League as the critics' favourites for relegation. And initially it looked as if they would be proved right, as Morton lost their first three games. With Ritchie scoring Morton's solitary goal in each match, they were written off as a one-man team. But a victory against Dundee United at Tannadice, ironically without Andy, turned the tide, and Morton never looked back. In no way were they a one-man team, but it cannot be denied that without Ritchie, they might well have struggled to survive that season. As it was, they finished a comfortable seventh, and Ritchie walked away with the Sportswriters' Player of the Year Trophy. But it was Jim Holmes who won the supporters' award, a fitting reward for three seasons of tremendous dedication and consistency. On countless occasions people would come from all over the country ostensibly to see Ritchie, and leave the match raving about the 'wee left-back' and wondering why he wasn't in the Scotland side. In a team full of characters Andy Ritchie was of course the biggest of them all.

'I remember leading up to Andy being named Player of the Year and him saying to me, "Wee man, I know a couple of people that have voted for you. That could win it!"' But Jim knew that there could be only one winner of the big award. Ritchie had made such a sensational impression in Morton's first season with the big boys that there could be no other choice, but he was honoured to receive the supporters' award. 'My whole time at Morton was characterised by my relationship with the fans. They were great to me throughout my 12 years there. They were absolutely brilliant. I can't speak highly enough of them.'

Buoyed by their fine debut season in the Premier League, Benny Rooney felt that Morton were capable of securing a European place the following season, and the early part of the season saw 'Ton up with the leaders. Even so, it took the television companies until the middle of October to realise that Morton were in the Premier League, and then they couldn't get enough of them with Morton games being televised three weeks in a row. The first, against Rangers at Ibrox, ended 2–2, the next at Cappielow – watched by almost 20,000 – saw Morton beat reigning champions Celtic 1–0. The following week saw them comprehensively thrash Partick Thistle 4–1 at Firhill. Homer scored the first goal against the club

Holmes spectacularly heads away a certain goal in 1988.

and the manager who had let him go. His delight was unconcealed, and suddenly Scottish football woke up to the fact that there were new kids on the block. Driven on by powerhouse Bobby Thomson in midfield, and with Ritchie orchestrating everything, 'Ton went on a nine-match unbeaten League run, and topped the Premier League for two weeks. They were also fancied to do well in the Cups, and by December had reached the Scottish League Cup semi-final, after knocking out Kilmarnock on penalties after two pulsating quarter-final matches. With the sides level at 5–5 after extra-time, they were also level on penalties, and it fell to Homer to score the decisive winning penalty. In the semi they were drawn against Aberdeen, bossed by old St Mirren adversary Alex Ferguson. By this stage of the season, Morton had already defeated Aberdeen twice in the league, and were quietly fancied. But just when they needed a big performance, they unaccountably froze. Hampden nerves got to some of the players, and Aberdeen won 2–1. Morton's frustration was compounded when an equalizing 'goal' by Neil

Orr was disallowed for offside against a Morton player who was standing miles away from the play.

> *I went into that match really looking forward to Hampden's wide open spaces and motoring up and down the left flank, but early on Jimmy Miller got booked and I was moved into midfield directly up against Gordon Strachan. Nuff said!*

And sadly the season began to go downhill one week later at Cappielow against Rangers in a match that witnessed one of Scottish football's most controversial incidents. Late in the first half, with the game goalless, Bobby Thomson fouled Rangers legend Sandy Jardine. When Jardine picked himself up and remonstrated with Thomson their heads met, and Jardine went down clutching his forehead. A distraught Thomson, claiming his innocence, was red-carded, and his loss was significant. Rangers won the match 1–0, and the papers were full of accusations and counter-accusations for days afterwards. To this day most Morton fans will swear that Thomson was innocent, but he still made the head-butting gesture and as such deserved to walk. The incident detracted from a tremendous Jim Holmes performance, one that the *Daily Record*'s Jack Adams called 'the best full-back performance of the season'.

The Rangers match effectively derailed Morton's season, and they fell away in the League, despite again defeating Aberdeen for the third time that season just a few weeks after the League Cup semi-final defeat. Morton finished the season in sixth position, 12 points behind – ironically enough – Aberdeen, who took advantage of a stuttering Old Firm to take the title with the low total of 48 points. 'Ton were eliminated by Celtic in the Scottish Cup quarter-finals, and the season that had promised so much ended in disappointment. But Jim Holmes had cemented his reputation as one of the country's most reliable and consistent full-backs. So much so, that halfway through that season when a poll was taken among the Premier League managers for their best Premier League side, nine out of 10 managers voted for Jim. The missing vote belonged to his own manager, as they were not allowed to vote for their own players.

Yet there still wasn't a sniff of international recognition for Jim. Perhaps the fact that he was part-time, playing for an unfashionable side, worked against him. Yet even when Morton were one of the country's top sides, Homer was repeatedly ignored. With no disrespect intended to the full-backs who were turning out for Scotland at the time, it really must be considered an absolute travesty that Homer never won a cap. Jim himself is philosophical about the situation: 'It honestly never entered my head that I would be considered for Scotland. There was a story that Jock Stein watched me in a Renfrewshire Cup Final against St Mirren, but we lost 6–0!'

There were also occasional enquiries from bigger sides for Jim. Hibs and Celtic were rumoured to be interested, but nothing came of it, and Jim has no regrets anyway:

> *I absolutely loved playing for Morton. I used to travel to the home games with big Andy and when we drove down the motorway, and the Firth of Clyde came into view, that set me off. Then there would be a wee warm up at Cappielow, then lunch at the Tontine Hotel, then the match. It was a great life. We had a great dressing room, great patter. You gave out stick and got it back in return. There were no cliques, no big time charlies. And Benny Rooney and Mike Jackson were a great team. Mike was the joker, and Benny was a good man manager. Tactically, Benny never restricted me. He encouraged me at all times to go forward. And I was always more comfortable in the opponent's half of the field anyway.*

Although Jim was an excellent defender, his true strength was going forward. As Derek Collins says, he was a pure footballer. If Andy Ritchie set up a barrow load of goals in his time at Cappielow, then Homer made his fair share as well, with his overlapping runs down the flank. The 'Holmes shuffle' became his trademark, and he left more than one opponent bamboozled with his very own trick of running past the ball and flicking it away with his heel while in full flight.

> *I was never the type of defender who would hit his opponent hard and*

Holmes points the way against St
Mirren in a 2-0 defeat at Cappielow on
31 October 1981.

Holmes hoodwinks
Celtic's Mo Johnston.

Jim Holmes receiving the Morton Player of the Year trophy from Chairman Hugh Currie in 1979.

take player and ball. Hannibal was like that and I think I tried it for one game and ended up hurting myself more! Anyway, my interpretation of a good defender is one who makes the right decisions at the right time. I think when I played most managers preferred their defenders just to win the ball at all costs and if they could play a bit as well that was a bonus.

Season 1980–81 proved to be the last hurrah for Benny Rooney's fine Morton side. They failed to set the Premier League on fire as they had in their previous two seasons, but had a fine run in the Scottish Cup, reaching the semi-final. Matches involving Morton and Rangers have a history of controversy, and this one was no different. The talismanic Ritchie was left on the bench by Benny Rooney, as the manager feared a physical confrontation, which is exactly what transpired. A bruising first half saw referee McGinlay warn several players, but also ignore several unsavoury incidents. Morton had their traditional goal disallowed, before Rangers scored just before half time. The second half saw the game deteriorate into a series of feuds, and referee McGinlay called the two captains together to warn them that the next player to commit a foul would be sent off. Unfortunately Morton skipper Bobby Thomson failed to pass the message on. A few minutes later Homer committed his first foul of the match when he clipped 'Gers' Ally Dawson in an inocuous challenge. Referee McGinlay awarded a free kick to Rangers and astounded everyone by sending Homer off. Shortly afterwards Rangers scored again, then Andy Ritchie, on as a substitute, pulled one back with a penalty. But any chance 'Ton had was lost when Thomson was given a straight red card for a foul with 10 minutes left.

I was sitting in the dressing room with my head in my hands after I'd been red carded, and then the dressing room door burst open and big Thommo breezed in with a daft grin on his face and said: 'I just had to dae it wee man!' It was only then that he told me about the referee's warning. But then the big man never was much of a talker on the park.

Morton's card total of five yellow and two red cost them dear, with the SFA holding back bonus money for each card earned. Both clubs were roundly condemned in the press for their indiscipline. For Morton, it was a great chance lost against a poor Rangers side, and for Jim a huge personal disappointment.

Season 1982–83 saw the end of the minor miracle that Benny Rooney had achieved at Morton, and the team were relegated. Benny lost his job, and the following season, despite having three managers over the term, Morton won the first division, but the side had changed drastically, with the stars of the side like Ritchie, Orr, Thomson, Joe McLaughlin and Jim Tolmie having moved on. Even stalwarts like Hayes and Anderson had left the club. Homer remained, along with John McNeil, a constant reminder of the golden era. Jim agrees with Andy Ritchie that if Morton had been just a little more ambitious, then they could have achieved more under Benny Rooney.

We got the best out of the players that we had at our disposal, and perhaps if we had been a bit more ambitious and went full-time things could have been different. It's hard to attract good players to a part-time club. Unfortunately, when we sold our best players, some of the ones that came in weren't quite in the same class.

Jim himself remained part-time throughout his time at Morton, combining his football with his job as an engineer with Rolls-Royce.

During that title-winning season of 1983–84 Morton began with Alec Miller as manager. Miller left after a couple of months, to be replaced by caretaker Eddie Morrison, and then Tommy McLean came in for the tail end of the season. By the time they returned to the Premier League for season 1984–85 there was yet another manager at the helm in the shape of Tommy McLean's brother Willie. Morton were relegated after only one season back in the Premier, as they endured a nightmare season under the dour McLean. One of the high spots of this period for Jim was the opportunity to play with Jim Duffy, who won the Scottish Player of the Year Award in 1985, despite the fact that Morton conceded 100 League goals that season. As Jim says with considerable understatement: 'No doubt about it, Duff was a one-man defence that season.'

In 1985 Morton football club at last got the manager they deserved when Allan McGraw was appointed, with the express aim of returning the club to the Premier League. For Jim's part he counts himself a member of the Allan McGraw fan club. 'I really enjoyed playing under Allan. He's a great guy who always commanded total respect. He was a man who gave everything for Morton, and ended up being treated unfairly when he was more or less forced out.'

Within two seasons Allan had achieved his aim, and Homer took his total of Division One championship medals to three in 1987 when he skippered Morton to the first division title. Homer weighed in with his best-ever season's total of three goals, all of them vital. For one match he even did a fair impersonation of Andy Ritchie, with a swerving free-kick goal from 20 yards. The goal helped secure a 3–2 victory, and was straight out of Andy's repertoire. 1987 must rank as one of the most memorable seasons of Jim's career. His season was complete (or so he thought) when he won belated international honours. Jim captained the Scotland semi-professional side in a round robin tournament involving sides outwith the top league of Scotland, England, Holland, and Italy. Jim played in all three matches, and the Scotland side gave a good account of themselves, defeating Holland. At 33, Jim thought things couldn't get any better, but he was wrong. His fellow pros voted him first division player of the year for 1986–87, a fitting reward for a tremendous 10 years at Cappielow.

Sadly, the following season in the Premier League found Morton wanting, and they were again relegated. Jim had now reached that stage of his career when thoughts were turning to the possibility of a testimonial match. But before this could happen, Falkirk enquired about Jim's availability. Surprisingly, Morton didn't discourage them, and Jim found himself mulling over a move to Falkirk. A fee of £10,000 was involved, but many Morton fans thought the club were being a little disingenuous in taking money for a great servant who had cost them nothing, although Jim was able to negotiate a favourable settlement. With 516 appearances, Jim was for many years the club's record appearance holder, and is now number three in the all-time list behind Derek Collins and David Wylie.

My one regret about leaving Morton is that I didn't know I was playing my last match for them. I would have liked the opportunity to say thanks and goodbye to the fans, because they had been great to me over the years. However, a few weeks after I left I played against Morton for Falkirk and they gave me a great reception from them.

Homer served Falkirk for two seasons, and was pleased to play under Jim Duffy in the latter's short spell as manager. During his time at Brockville Jim won two supporters' player of the year awards, and the club just missed out on promotion to the Premier League. Jim left Falkirk in 1989 and then played with Alloa for a spell before joining Arbroath, who were managed by his friend Ian Gibson. Jim helped out with coaching at Gayfield, and also picked up the obligatory club player of the year awards. At 36, he still felt he could play another couple of seasons, but the trip to Arbroath, coupled with his nine to five job, proved too much, and Jim decided to hang up his boots. In 18 seasons as a professional, Jim had played over 600 matches.

After retirement he was offered posts coaching Hibs and Celtic youth sides, but preferred to help run his son Graeme's boys club side, which he did for five years. His time there has reaped dividends, as several of the boys eventually went to senior clubs.

Nowadays, with Jim approaching his half century, he still looks as fit as ever, and still plays five-a-sides and for charity outfit Dukla Pumpherston. The man who was recently voted Morton's fifth-best player ever still looks capable of motoring up the left flank, producing the famous shuffle, and setting another goal chance up. And happily the Holmes name lives on in Scottish football, with Jim's son Graeme a promising midfielder with Dundee United. 'I repeatedly tell Graeme how lucky I was to have had a career in football, and especially with a great club like Morton. I tell him that it could be worse. He might have to work for a living!'

Morton playing statistics: (League, League Cup, Scottish Cup)

Season	Appearances	Goals
1976–77	46	2
1977–78	45 +1sub	0
1978–79	45	0
1979–80	43	2
1980–81	42	0
1981–82	42	0
1982–83	43	0
1983–84	48	0
1984–85	39	1
1985–86	38	1
1986–87	44	3
1987–88	41	0

Chapter 7

Andy Ritchie
Genius

Let's nail the myth straight away. Andy Ritchie was a team player. 137 goals and countless assists in seven seasons at Morton tells us so. And lest there is any doubt, many of his teammates tell us so too. Newspaper editors love to pigeonhole players. That's why Andy was a gift for the journalists who unfairly dubbed him the 'idle idol'. When Sir Alex Ferguson described Andy as 'an overweight genius' in his autobiography, it was typical of the back-handed compliments that have haunted Andy throughout his playing career, and indeed subsequently. Andy himself is tired of the clichéd portrayal that unimaginative writers have attached to him. As Benny Rooney, the man who brought him to Cappielow, says, 'The idle idol reputation was a bit unfair. When I had Andy on his own he was a good trainer, it was only in a group situation that he lapsed a little.'

Perhaps the time is now right for a reassessment of Andy's career. Andy Ritchie was a supremely gifted individual who triumphed in a team game. He was at once part of the team, but his wonderful talent elevated him to a much higher plane. He had it all. He was a giant of a man, but his balance, ball control, passing ability and shooting prowess were unsurpassed. Okay, he didn't run about any more than he had to, and he didn't tackle an awful lot. So what? He didn't have to. Call him a maverick if you like, but his lineage can be traced through all the

Andy Ritchie
in 1979.

great Scottish players from Hughie Gallacher to Jim Baxter. Like them, he had that touch of arrogance and faith in his own ability that set him apart from other mere mortals.

Andy Ritchie was born in 1956 in Glasgow and spent his early life in the Calderpark region. His family later moved to Bellshill and as Andy's father was a Motherwell supporter, he took the young Andy to a lot of their matches. The excellent sides of the late 1960s, including John Martis, Bobby and Willie McCallum, and John Goldthorpe, were his early heroes. On leaving school, Andy's chosen career path was mining engineering, a path which very quickly met a dead end, as he realised it wasn't for him. Football was his passion. He played for his school team, where Craig Brown was his headmaster, and juvenile for Bellshill YM.

Basically like most other young lads I just played football all the time. If I couldn't rustle up a game with other kids, I'd be away by myself, always with a ball. I suppose I was born with a bit of a gift, but I was always working on my technique and ability. Not only that, in my head

Andy Ritchie nets a penalty against Airdrie in April 1978 to clinch promotion for Morton.

as well. I believe that a big percentage of football is played in your head, and I had a vivid imagination! I also lived near Jimmy Johnstone, remember, so he was always a reminder of what could be achieved.

Andy was 14 when he first realised that football clubs were interested in him. He played trials with Manchester United, Coventry, and Everton, and spent two months with Middlesborough.

I was homesick in Middlesborough after three days, and through the grapevine I heard that Celtic were interested. As a kid you have hopes and dreams and aspirations that one day you'll be good enough, but deep down you never really think that it will happen. It always happens to somebody else. I was a bit of a late starter. English clubs used to hold trials up here, and all the scouts would organise the best boys and hold trials on a Sunday. Clubs like West Brom, Crystal Palace and Leeds would be there. I was never, ever invited to any of those trials. Three guys from my team Bellshill YM were there one day, but there was a man short that day, and my dad told me to go along and make the numbers up. After 20 minutes I got taken off, and I got back on for the last 15 minutes. I only found out years later that the reason I'd been taken off after 20 minutes was because the Middlesborough coach was there and he knew the place was hoachin' with scouts and wanted me out of their sight. Middlesborough had first option on me and that was the reason I'd been taken off. I just thought I'd been having a poor game. It was almost as if Benny Rooney was the manager and the number 11 board was being held up… again! But at the end of the match before I got to the car park I'd been approached by the Manchester United and Celtic scouts, and by the time I got home the Rangers scout was in my mother's house.

Andy chose not to go back to Middlesborough, but still had his pick of big clubs. 'I could have signed for Rangers. I was training with them on a Tuesday

On-the-spot Andy slides in another penalty for Morton, this time in February 1979 in a 1–1 Scottish Cup third-round draw with St Johnston. The goalkeeper is Andy Geoghegan.

night and Celtic on a Thursday, but I went to Celtic because they were more organised, their structure was better.'

Andy joined the Celtic ground staff in 1971 aged 15, and followed the then tried and tested route of being farmed out to junior football. In Kenny Dalglish's case, it was Cumbernauld United. Andy went to Kirkintilloch Rob Roy. There he made a huge impression, scoring 35 goals in 18 matches, including five in his first match. At 17 Andy signed professional forms for Celtic, and he made an immediate impact in the reserves. Everything was happening quickly for Andy, but in retrospect he thinks it may have been too quick.

I wasn't achieving anything mentally, I wasn't growing up mentally. Physically yes, mentally no. I then hit a brick wall and didn't know how to fix it. I believed that I should have been in the first team, but my high expectations weren't backed up by my performances. I developed an attitude and wouldn't do what I was told. There was a two-year spell which wasn't good. All I needed was a tad of humility, but it was the arrogance of youth. If Jock Stein had been there he might have sorted me out. But he had been in a car crash and Parkhead was in turmoil without him. Players were leaving and I thought I was better than the replacements. When Jock did come back I had lost focus.

Andy managed half a dozen first-team appearances in 1975–76, but in October 1976 he took the decision to move to Morton.

*Benny [Rooney] had only just stopped playing, and I remember playing against him a couple of times, and he obviously remembered me. He was very persuasive and sold Morton to me. Of course, I could I have stayed with Celtic. There was a four-year deal on the table from Celtic, and I turned it down. Bad, bad, **bad** move!*

Of the many myths that have grown up around Andy, one of the strongest is of his love/hate relationship with Jock Stein.

All that stuff with big Jock has been exaggerated a bit. For his part I think it was more frustration at my attitude. I had that arrogant side to me and I couldn't be told. He rated me as a player, and was always trying to get me back into the fold. There was nothing Jock didn't know and nothing he couldn't do. Right up until the day I signed for Morton he tried to get me to stay. Can you imagine it? A four-year deal on the table, and I turned down possibly the greatest Scottish manager ever. I'll never forget when he finally gave up on me. He gave a disgusted aaargch! shrugged his shoulders and walked out the room.

Andy came to Morton just at the right time. The club had steadily gone downhill since the halcyon days of the 1960s, and had failed to gain a place in the promised land that was the much vaunted Premier League. Enter Benny Rooney, a dynamic, ambitious young manager who would galvanise a stagnating club, and for an all too brief period give Morton fans a team to be proud of. Benny had been at Morton for just a few months when he put the feelers out for Andy.

Celtic, as always seemed to be the case after Ronnie Simpson retired, were looking for a goalkeeper. Roy Baines had been outstanding for Morton for several seasons. Roy moved to Parkhead, and Andy came the other way as makeweight in the deal. Morton also received £10,000. That last part is worth repeating. Morton received £10,000. Celtic were actually giving Morton money to take Andy Ritchie off their hands. Now Roy Baines is indisputably one of Morton's best-ever goalkeepers, arguably second only to Jimmy Cowan, but Benny Rooney must have been rubbing his hands in glee at the thought of bringing Andy to Cappielow. But could Benny have known just how great a signing it would turn out to be?

Andy was the most talented player that I ever managed. He could do everything. When I took over at Morton I had a team full of workers and I signed Andy to give us that extra something. I wanted him on the ball making things happen. And he certainly did that for us. For three or four seasons he was incredible. His dead ball skills and passing ability were second to none. He really was the cream on the cake.

Andy made a fairly quiet Morton debut in October at Cappielow against Clydebank. He impressed with his dribbling and close control, which was excellent for such a big guy. He also gave a sign of things to come with a couple of free-kicks that were capably dealt with by the Bankies goalie. A few of the Cappielow cognoscenti reckoned he was a star of the future, and by the time of his next home match when he scored two goals against Montrose, few were in any doubt that he was a star of the present. His double against Montrose included one direct from a free-kick. Up until then, most Scottish fans' exposure to free-kick goals was via grainy black and white images from the 1970 Mexico World Cup, when Pelé, Rivelino et al had held us spellbound into the wee hours of the morning.

I always knew that I had a talent for striking the ball in a certain way, and I would spend time after training practicing my passing and hitting free-kicks. I went over to Germany in 1974 to support Scotland in the World Cup, and I happened to catch a Brazilian training session. And that was all they were doing, hitting free-kick after free-kick. And they had this big cardboard wall, the first time I had seen anything like it and they were swerving the ball around it. Just sitting there watching them made me wish I could get on the park with them.

And so, working on the old adage 'If you can't join them, beat them', free-kicks became an integral part of Andy's game. Over his seven years at Morton he would frequently astonish fans, teammates, and opponents alike with his astonishing dead ball prowess.

In his first season at Cappielow Benny Rooney moulded a promising side around the talents of Andy. A tremendous unbeaten run of games secured them fourth place in the League, and Andy finished with 22 goals in 27 appearances. 'I had several seasons of full-time training behind me, and when I joined Morton I was as fit as I've ever been, and so I hit the ground running.' But Morton fans were unaware that they had been close to losing their new hero soon after his arrival:

I'd only played eight games for Morton, and Celtic were willing to pay up to £175,000 to bring me back on the proviso that Morton took the money and said I'd only been at Cappielow on loan. But Hal Stewart said no, I'll get a million for him, and that was that.

The start of the 1977–78 season saw Hearts and Dundee installed as favourites for promotion. Both sides were full-time and more fashionable than part-time Morton. But no one had read the script to the Morton players. They dominated the League from day one, with the Ritchie/ Mark McGhee combination on fire, and Andy was thrilled to play alongside his old hero John Goldthorpe. The football was terrific with Andy as chief conductor.

My brief was just to get on the ball and make the team play. Benny Rooney at that time was one of the best young managers in the game. He had good contacts in the game and knew what he wanted, and he knew

Scottish football. I got the feeling after a couple of months that something was happening. He gave me more or less a free role, within reason. For myself, all I wanted to do was score goals and make things happen. I just went out to enjoy myself, make the team play, and tried to entertain.

One of the more memorable matches in season 1977–78 was at Cappielow against Hearts. There was an air of expectancy around the ground as the sides took the field. Hearts had comprehensively defeated 'Ton 3–0 in the League Cup only three days previously, and this was to be the game where the Edinburgh aristocrats would put the poor relations from Greenock in their place, and finish their challenge. It didn't quite work out like that as Morton took the game to Hearts from the off, and produced a scintillating display of attacking football. Morton led 3–0 at half-time, and the match was effectively over. Well not quite, as Hearts quickly pulled two goals back after the interval, but Morton were not to be denied and from a Ritchie corner, the much maligned Roddy Hutchison bulleted a header past the Hearts goalie. Morton then made it 5–2 before Hearts pulled a third goal back near the end.

A jubilant Morton side and supporters celebrated a performance that signalled that Benny Rooney's side had come of age. The most surprising thing about the match was the absence of Andy's name from the scoresheet, but the most significant factor was that he had set up four of Morton's goals, proving that when he played a deeper role he could be just as effective. Morton never looked back after this match and promotion and the championship were eventually secured against Airdrie in the second to last game, with Andy clinching victory with a last-minute penalty to make the score 3–1.

Despite Morton's fine performance in winning the First Division championship in 1978, the doubters were still writing them off for their debut Premier League season. Initially they did struggle, but soon found their feet. Morton fans could certainly be forgiven a certain smugness as the season dawned. They knew exactly what was to be unleashed on the unsuspecting Premier League. Andy gave warning of his intentions for the Premier League in a pre-season friendly at home

Andy Ritchie: a giant but with perfect balance.

to Watford. A 40-yard howitzer of a free-kick just about uprooted the goal on its way into the net. This match probably was the start of Andy's 'goalden' era, when he was scoring goals that no one else could. He was trying things that no other player even thought about, and they were coming off. Long-range shots and free-kicks were flying in from all angles, and suddenly the Scottish press realised that they had a star in their midst. Unfortunately it was too late for the Scottish national side, who had suffered in the World Cup at the hands – or should that be the feet – of Peru's version of Ritchie, Teofilo Cubillas. Scotland goalie Alan Rough had stood rooted to the spot as Cubillas rifled two rockets past him in 1978.

It was good preparation for Roughie as Andy would do it to him on a regular basis in the Premier League. But according to Andy he could have been in Argentina along with Roughie.

Ally McLeod wanted to take me to Argentina but the SFA committee said it wouldn't look good taking a part-time player. He said he wanted me in the squad although he wouldn't use me all the time, but I was ready for international football.

Morton's first season in the Premier League was an unqualified success, and despite the all-round excellence of Benny Rooney's side, there can be no argument that Andy Ritchie's goals and all-round play were the dominant factors in keeping 'Ton in the Premier League in that first season. Andy was the League's top scorer with a string of sensational efforts. At the end of the season, although new Scotland manager Jock Stein could ignore him, no one else could and Andy walked away with the Football Writers' player of the year award for 1979. Celebrated football writer Hugh Taylor said at the time: 'His outrageous gifts border on the genius.' Andy is refreshingly candid and modest about why he was such a sensation.

The whole country had endured a horrendous World Cup in Argentina. Football in Scotland needed a lift, and I was there in the right place at the right time. The press had to find something different to write about. Some-thing that was new and fresh, and that was when it all started for me.

There were still those that doubted him though.

It was always as if both myself and Morton always had to go that extra mile to prove ourselves. With Morton it was, 'Well they've done well to get in the promotion race, but Hearts and Dundee will sort them out.' Then it was 'well they've done well to win promotion, but the big boys will sort them out.' And so it went on, but we consistently proved the doubters wrong. We had a great spirit. And it was the same with me. I constantly had to prove myself. And then the press built this persona of me, the idle idol thing, and it just grew arms and legs.

Andy came to the fore just when work-rate began to out-distance talent in many supposedly knowledgeable football people's minds. Just as his compatriots south of the border, like Stan Bowles, Rodney Marsh and Frank Worthington, were being usurped by 'team' players who took the man first and asked questions later, Andy too, suffered from his supposed laziness.

I can't deny I loved the adulation, and my first few years at Morton were fantastic, but I wanted international football, and that meant full-time football. Morton made noises about it, but it never happened and looking back that was a mistake, although we achieved a hell of a lot with what we had. So, I was constantly looking for a move. When I joined Morton I looked on it as taking a step back to take two steps forward, and all I was looking for was the move I had been promised when I joined.

So Andy was constantly badgering Morton for a move but a combination of his image and Morton looking for too much money denied Andy the transfer he craved. Bids were certainly made for him. Hearts bid £200,000, as did Sheffield

Wednesday, managed by Jack Charlton. Liverpool also enquired but were put off by Morton's asking price.

Andy was at the peak of his powers in 1979 as Morton powered to the top of the Premier League. He was the finest attacker in the country, the only player apart from Dalglish who could rival the best of the Continentals, yet he couldn't get a look in for Scotland. Stein compromised slightly, and capped Andy once for the Scottish League, and as an overage player for the Under-21s. Andy scored in the League match but never got the call for the full national side. Morton's second season in the Premier League provided many highs and lows and more memorable Ritchie moments. One of the disappointments was the League Cup semi-final defeat against Aberdeen. Morton had already beaten the Dons twice that season, and should have gone into the match full of confidence, but some of the players froze and Morton lost 2–1. Andy stills feels the disappointment keenly.

We really should have beaten Aberdeen that day. It was probably one of the few times that as a team we didn't do ourselves justice. Aberdeen got let off the hook that day and they knew it. The game was over before we started to play.

In Morton's third season in the Premier League they reached the Scottish Cup semi-final, a match that would provide a defining moment in Andy's career. The 1981 cup run provided Andy's finest and worst memories of his time at Cappielow. He had scored a wonder goal against Aberdeen in the fourth round, and Morton faced Rangers in the semi-final. Benny Rooney didn't make too many mistakes as Morton boss, but his decision to leave Andy on the bench that day was a costly one for Morton. Benny afterwards explained his decision:

It was one of the hardest decisions that I ever had to make in football. It's easy to say in hindsight that I should have played Andy, but I knew it would be a physical match, and decided to bring in a different type of player to Andy, and after all, Rangers left out Davie Cooper. But I made the decision at the time, and you live or die by it.

Andy himself claims that Benny Rooney never gave that reason to him, saying merely that he had decided to leave him out of the starting XI.

To be honest I wasn't playing well. I was playing well in the cup, but I was struggling for consistency in the league. When Benny told me on the Friday that he was putting me on the bench, I thought he was kidding. I remember thinking that he would phone me on the Friday night and tell me he had changed his mind. I didn't take it too well at the time. If Benny had given me a valid reason at the time, like I wasn't playing well, or it was tactical it would have been easier to take. But he never really gave me

Morton's Andy Ritchie confronts Celtic full-back Andy Lynch at Cappielow Park, Greenock, 20 October 1979.

Andy Ritchie scores from the penalty spot to put Morton into a 2–0 lead against Rangers at Cappielow on Saturday 6 October 1980. Rangers fought back to get a 2–2 draw.

a valid reason. He said afterwards that he didn't really want to leave me out and that was why he couldn't answer me at that time.

In the event Rooney was proven right about the physical side of the match, which wasn't helped by inconsistent refereeing. Morton were not a particularly physical side. Morton had their usual goal disallowed and lost the match 2–1, and had two players ordered off. Andy came off the bench, almost inevitably scoring with a penalty, but it was too late to make a real difference. Morton had blown a great chance to reach their first Scottish Cup final in 33 years.

Looking back on it, it wasn't like the semi against Aberdeen when we went in cold and froze a bit. We had gained the experience to win

Andy's greatest goal? Morton v Aberdeen in the Scottish Cup in 1981.

matches like that so obviously it was a huge disappointment. I know I had let Benny down at times, but I felt he let me down that day. Unfortunately I wasn't mature enough to accept it and get on with it.

The side began to break up shortly afterwards, with Jim Tolmie, Neil Orr and Bobby Thomson all moving on. It was always felt the big man would follow them out the door. He had actually first asked for a move on the eve of Morton's first season in the Premier League.

Whenever a player left Morton for a bigger club, nobody resented it, because we were all only too delighted for them. Because of the spirit in the dressing room we never thought why him and not me? After all, we're all in the game to better ourselves and play at as high a level as possible.

Somehow the move never materialised and Andy's form suffered. Disillusionment set in when it became evident that no big club was prepared to spend big money on a player who wasn't willing to conform to the accepted practice of drowning in his own sweat. Two more undistinguished seasons followed. He had averaged 27 goals a season in his first four seasons at Cappielow, but that had fallen to 11 by 1982. In his last season at Morton Andy started only 16 League games, and Morton were relegated. Andy admits now that he was disillusioned, but didn't have the wherewithal to do anything about it.

The game came too easily to me, and that's why I only played till I was 27. The game just happened for me, if it didn't happen a lot of times I didn't know why. When I ran into a bad spell I didn't know how to make it better. Guys like Jim Holmes did. They worked harder, they knuckled down. That's why they had long careers. I didn't do that. And that's to my detriment.

Teammate Jim Holmes says: 'If Andy had left Morton earlier when he was at his peak, he would have played much longer. But Morton held on and held on.' Andy agrees:

By the time I got to the end of my spell there I had lost the eye for the game, and I needed to move on. That was what had been promised to me when I joined, but it should have happened sooner. I had taken my eye off the ball. I needed full-time training for a start. I wasn't receiving incoming phone calls. You could put it that way.

But when Andy finally did leave Morton it was for a similar-sized club, Motherwell, the club he had supported as a boy. The legendary Jock Wallace signed him, and Andy tried hard to get himself fit, and actually got on very well with the ex-Rangers manager. 'Big Jock got me fit but wouldn't let me play. If I spent more than a couple of seconds on the ball he'd be screaming at me to get rid of it.'

Andy bamboozles McLeish before scoring against Aberdeen in 1981.

Then Bobby Watson took over from Wallace and after 13 games and four goals, Andy moved on again. He had brief spells with Clydebank and East Stirling, but by now he had let his fitness go. He moved on to Albion Rovers, and began season 1984–85 as player-coach. By this time, however, Andy knew the game was up, and after only three games he quit. Totally disenchanted with football, he had accepted a job outside football in London, and one of the greatest talents ever seen in Scottish football was lost to the game at the age of 28. In the 20 years since he retired, Andy has returned frequently to the game he graced, but never as a player. He has been assistant manager of Hamilton, and coached St Mirren and Celtic youngsters. But possibly his greatest enjoyment has been in his role as talent spotter. He has travelled all over Europe in his capacity as chief scout for a number of clubs including Derby and Aston Villa. And of course it was while working in that role for Celtic that he helped bring Paul Lambert and Pierre Van Hooijdonk to the club. Now older and wiser, Andy knows he made mistakes.

As he shoots past Celtic goalkeeper Pat Bonner, Andy Ritchie scores Morton's opening goal at Cappielow on Saturday 20 October 1980.

Where does one start to pick the best of Andy's goals? Was it the long-range rocket against Watford, or the free-kick that was shown all around Britain against the hapless Rough? Andy lined Roughie's wall up for him, then cheekily peeked round it before placing the ball in the top corner of the net. Or perhaps it was when he did what Pelé couldn't do and scored from the halfway line against Dundee United, or maybe it was the one that didn't stand against Celtic at Parkhead when he powered home a 30-yarder into the teeth of a gale. Andy's own favourite is when he chipped giant Rangers 'keeper Peter McCloy.

One of the really frustrating things about Andy's career is that so little of it is captured for posterity. Andy played in the days before saturated television coverage, and the television companies just tended to show Rangers or Celtic every week. Consequently, only a couple of Andy's wonderful goals are available to view. Thankfully, one goal that was recorded is perhaps his greatest. Morton against Aberdeen, Scottish Cup fourth round, February 1981. The big man wasn't having the best of seasons, but he reminded us all of his genius that day. Morton were Aberdeen's bogey team at that time. Under Alex Ferguson the Dons were just beginning their domination of Scottish football. They were reigning champions, and feared no one, except Morton who had beaten them several times in the preceding few seasons. As Alex McLeish freely admits, they, and particularly goalkeeper Jim Leighton, were terrified of Andy. This was evident when, after about 20 minutes of the match, Andy received the ball with his back to the Aberdeen goal 20 yards out. Behind him, defending deep, were left-back Doug Considine, McLeish, Willie Miller and Leighton, in other words three-fifths of what was soon to be Scotland's defence. The pass was really no more than a hopeful punt from John Marr, but Andy took the ball on his chest and flicked the ball up and over his head. As he pivoted Considine performed a fair impersonation of a rubber man and slipped, probably out of terror, and McLeish and Miller tried to close Andy down. On the face of it, it was text-book defending by the Scotland central defenders, but in reality their faces were transfixed like a pair of rabbits caught in the glare of car headlights. Leighton hopped about like a toothless, bandy-legged cat on hot bricks. Completely unfazed, Andy controlled the ball on the turn and curved the ball with the outside of his right boot around the two defenders and past Leighton into the only uncovered area of the goal. Cappielow erupted. It was a special goal even by Andy's standards. It was the only goal of the match. To put the goal into perspective, Aberdeen did not lose another Scottish Cup match until 1985. After that match they won the cup for three years in a row, probably because they managed to avoid Morton! Andy regularly gave Rough and Leighton nightmares with his shooting accuracy. Probably the game that started it all was in Morton's first season in the Premier League in a match at Cappielow, when Andy curled a free-kick past Leighton from way out on the left touchline. From then on it became a regular occurrence.

Mark McGhee remembers the effect Andy had on his old mentor at Aberdeen, Alex Ferguson. 'Big Andy worried the life out of Fergie, especially at dead balls. In all my career I think only Glenn Hoddle and Manny Kaltz rival Andy as an accomplished striker of the ball.'

It almost goes without saying that Andy enjoyed an incredible rapport with the Morton fans. His humour was legendary. He often took time out for a wisecrack, and to call him an entertainer is an understatement. The Morton fans adored him, and still do. In a recent poll Andy was overwhelmingly voted the greatest-ever Morton player. There's no doubt that if he had been playing today, Andy would be a superstar. In a business where David Beckham has become one of the most famous men on the planet, and made untold millions through his talents, what price Andy Ritchie? What price genius? Andy, thanks for the memories.

Morton playing statistics: (League, League Cup, Scottish Cup)

Season	Appearances	Goals
1976–77	27 +1sub	22
1977–78	45	26
1978–79	45	29
1979–80	44	27
1980–81	35 +5subs	11
1981–82	29 +2subs	7
1982–83	22 +8subs	6

Chapter 8

Rowan Alexander
Super Ro!

As iconic goal celebrations go, Rowan Alexander's forward roll may not quite be in the same class as Denis Law's iconic one arm in the air, or Jürgen Klinsman's swallow dive, but for many Morton fans it summed up an era at Cappielow. Rowan performed that forward roll well over 100 times in a Morton jersey, and for almost 10 years it was a much anticipated and appreciated sight at Cappielow.

From Rowan's very first match for Morton in 1986 when he performed his first forward roll, his unstinting energy and enthusiasm endeared him to the Morton fans. His popularity is such that in a recent poll Rowan was voted the sixth greatest Morton player of all time. Rowan says of his time at Cappielow:

> It was the best 10 years of my football career. I got off to a great start and the fans took to me straight away. It was a two way thing. They appreciated the effort I put in, and I appreciated the support and backing they gave me.

And as for the forward roll? 'It was something I had done when I was at Brentford, and I just made up my mind that I would carry it on at Morton.'

Rowan was born in Ayr in 1961. He came from a farming background, his father moving the family to Carlisle when he took over as manager of a pig farm. A bit of a late developer in football terms, Rowan didn't really begin playing seriously until he was 13 or 14, but developed very quickly. He was playing at Under-18 level aged 14 for Annan Athletic. At this stage, because of his age, he was fairly small in stature and often played as a winger. But living on a farm did wonders for his physique and technique.

> *I can remember as a kid on the farm practicing in the yard all year long, even winter time. I erected some halogen floodlights in the yard just to play and practice every night possible in order to better myself. I did all the mucking out of the pigs, just to build me up physically because I was always slightly built, but I ended up a strong little bugger. I never really practiced to be a striker, but what I was doing was working on my touch, and improving on turning and receiving balls off the walls and moving away with it. This routine improved my game immensely and helped me realise my dream of becoming a professional footballer. Sometimes I think that this type of dedication to improving skills has gone out of the modern game, and perhaps young players have lost the willingness to work hard to improve their ability.*

Still aged only 14 Rowan was cheered off the park on the shoulders of teammates after scoring the two goals that brought Annan victory in an Under-18 cup final. He was on his way, and after trials aged 15 with Bury and Aston Villa, he spent time with Carlisle and Coventry. Carlisle manager Bobby Moncur wanted to sign Rowan, but Queen of the South were also interested. Perhaps as an omen of what was to come, Rowan asked his great Uncle Peter for advice. Uncle Peter just happened to be Peter Scott, chairman of Morton FC and former president of the SFA. Rowan's uncle advised him to sign for Queens, 'So we can keep an eye on you.' It was sage advice as Rowan became a hero at Palmerston, scoring 78 goals in just four seasons, averaging a goal every two games. Rowan's goalscoring feats eventually attracted bigger clubs. In 1983 he was transferred to St Mirren, managed by Ricki McFarlane. Unfortunately,

Rowan Alexander (left) displays his prodigious heading ability with yet another goal.

things didn't quite work out at Love Street for Rowan. During his spell there he broke an ankle, and an arm, and managed only 13 full appearances. When Alex Miller took over as manager in 1983 Rowan was deemed surplus to requirements and transferred to Brentford, managed by Frank McLintock. Again, this move was less than successful, and as Rowan admits he was struggling for consistency at this stage in his career, as he came to terms with full-time football. Towards the end of season 1985–86 Rowan was informed by McLintock that his contract wouldn't be renewed.

> *I was devastated, but had to pick myself up and proceeded to write letters to various clubs in Scotland. Remaining full time was a priority but there were no offers on the table. I had made up my mind to return to the family business, when Allan McGraw made contact with me, and invited me to training with Morton. I went down to Greenock on the Thursday*

prior to the season kicking off on the Saturday, so preparation and timing were not ideal. But after speaking to Allan I had no doubts about signing. It was part time football but I had no option really, as the man was so impressive.

Rowan made the bench for the first match of the season at Cappielow against Clyde.

I knew I would be involved at some stage, and sure enough when George Anderson was injured after about half an hour I was told by the gaffer to warm up. The crowd applauded, but for George, not me, a virtual unknown at that time.

The precarious nature of a footballer's career was never better illustrated than with this substitution. George Anderson, a great servant for Morton with over 300 games to his credit, never played first-team football again, but for Rowan, it was the start of something special. It didn't take Rowan long to make an impact. After an hour the match was deadlocked at 0–0, and Rowan, who clearly wasn't match fit, was easing himself into the match. Morton won a corner and when the ball came over Rowan peeled off his marker and, despite running away from the goal, instinctively adjusted his movement, executing a perfect bicycle kick into the net. The forward roll followed, and the Morton fans had a new goalscoring hero to rival manager McGraw. Morton won the match 3–0, and for Rowan it was the start of one of the best seasons of his career and 10 great years at Cappielow. He started the next match against Kilmarnock and scored again in a 2–2 draw. Allan McGraw himself was confident he had signed the player that could fire his side back into the Premier League. He had been a long-term admirer of Rowan, and had been monitoring his situation for some time. His intuition was proved right. As the season went on Rowan's confidence grew, along with the team as a whole, and successive 5–2 victories over Partick and Queen of the South yielded five goals for Rowan including a hat-trick against Queens – a header, a penalty and an opportunist strike. Rowan then followed that up with the vital winning goal in a 2–1 victory over Airdrie. Strikers thrive on confidence and Rowan was no different.

My name was in the papers again, and what a lift it gave me. It turned out to be a great first season. The games came thick and fast, and I was floating in games, relishing the next one to come along. I was going into games full of confidence, and everything I touched turned to gold. I was trying things in matches that others wouldn't dream of.

A tremendous run from November during which they lost only three out of 24 matches resulted in Morton lying one point ahead of Dunfermline with one match

Rowan Alexander celebrating what he does best – scoring goals.

Rowan Alexander shows trademark determination and concentration in driving rain to score against Dumbarton in 1994.

left. 'Ton needed to win their last match against Airdrie as leaders Dunfermline faced relegated Montrose, and were expected to win easily. Morton lost 1–0 to Airdrie, but unbelievably Montrose beat Dunfermline 1–0, and Morton were First Division Champions.

> *I couldn't believe what had happened but it crowned off a marvellous season, not just for me, but for Allan McGraw. The man is a legend, a man you could not help wanting to do well for. He was, and still is, hugely respected in the footballing world. Allan McGraw should not be out of football at all, at any time.*

Rowan Alexander's testimonial game against Falkirk in 1995.

Rowan with
his children at
his
testimonial
game.

At the end of a great first season at Morton Rowan had scored 26 goals, making him top goalscorer in the League, and won the club's Player of the Year Award. Several matches had been won during the season by narrow margins with Rowan's goals being vital, none more so than in narrow victories against Partick Thistle, Brechin and Queen of the South at crucial stages of the season. Rowan was also nominated for the First Division Player of the Year, losing out to teammate and captain Jim Holmes. Rowan was delighted for his skipper.

I didn't grudge Jim the award, he certainly deserved it. He was a model pro and a big influence on me. He led by example. He had a tremendous attitude and was very fit. Jim got his just rewards that season when he won the Division One player of the year. I was happy just to be nominated. I was in good company with Homer, John Watson and Norrie McCathie. I actually didn't think it could get any better than it was.

Rowan was wrong. He was named in a Scotland squad along with Holmes for a tournament involving the national sides from Scotland, England, Italy and Holland. For Holmes in particular it was belated international recognition, long overdue. Jim Holmes himself is in no doubt about the importance of Rowan Alexander to Morton.

Rowan was a great signing by Allan McGraw. I remember one particular match against Partick Thistle when we won the first division in 1987. It was one of those dour matches with hardly any scoring chances. I think we only had one chance the whole game, and up popped Rowan and that was three points in the bag. It was a vital win, and Rowan was like that. If we were struggling we knew we could knock the ball up to him, and he would hold it up or knock it on. He was a very aggressive player and he was brilliant in the air. Rowan was a great player to have on your side.

Morton and Rowan began the next season full of optimism that they would do well in the Premier League. As Rowan says: 'We had players with good reputations in the game, and we had a good mixture of experience and youth.' There was David Wylie, a promising young goalkeeper, fiery midfielder Tommy Turner, gifted individual John McNeil and of course Jim Holmes, provider of many of Rowan's goals with his surging runs forward from left-back. Sadly, the step up in class and the rigours of a 44-match League programme proved too much for 'Ton and they were relegated once more, suffering several drubbings. Despite this, Rowan enjoyed the experience of playing at Ibrox and Parkhead in front of huge crowds, and pitting his wits against internationals like Terry Butcher, Paul Hegarty and Willie Miller.

For Rowan, it had been a lifetime's ambition realised. He endured a disappointing season, managing only eight goals, although there was a nice memory of a 3–2 victory over Graeme Souness's Rangers. This was Morton's first victory against Rangers at Cappielow for almost 70 years, Rowan scoring with a header, out-jumping Terry Butcher, a feat in itself. Rowan would never again match the goalscoring exploits of his first season at Morton, but he became a steady, reliable figurehead, leading the forward line splendidly, consistently averaging a dozen goals a season, many of them crucial. He became the focal point of Allan McGraw's attractive team, watching a steady flow of talented youngsters come and go.

Over his nine seasons at Cappielow Rowan played with a number of different striking partners. Here's how he rates some of the strikers he played alongside in his 10 years there.

Dougie Robertson was my first strike partner. He wasn't the most mobile of players, but he complemented me well. He was a touch player who took a lot of the weight off me. I had one really good season with David McCabe. He was lightning quick, a different sort from Dougie all together! After Davie we had Alex Mathie for a couple of seasons and he was a quality goal scorer. Alex was good at getting in behind defences, benefiting from my knock ons. Derek Lilley was just a quality striker, a

Rowan Alexander receives a round of applause from the rest of the players in his testimonial game against Falkirk.

strong player who again, was adept at getting in behind defences. I enjoyed playing with all these guys, having to adapt my game to suit each individual.

Rowan's game did evolve over the years. He became much more than a mere goalscorer, taking on the role of the target man who brought others into the game. Derek Lilley in particular benefited from Rowan's promptings and Rowan himself feels that leading the line improved his game. Rowan's aerial ability was an outstanding feature of his game for a man who only stands 5ft 9in.

It is a gift definitely, but as a young player I worked hard on my technique and timing because that's the secret. I also worked hard to build up my calf muscles and worked hard on my physical presence. I was a midfielder as a youngster and Archie Gemmill was my favourite player, and I admired his all-action style and tried to emulate it.

For his own part Rowan credits Allan McGraw for making him a better player. 'As a striker himself, Allan certainly knew what he was talking about, and his advice and knowledge undoubtedly improved my overall game.'

Twenty-six goals in your first season at a club can do wonders for your popularity with the support, but Rowan struck up an almost immediate rapport with the Morton fans, largely due to his unbridled enthusiasm, and his willingness to run himself into the ground for the team. His popularity at Morton remained undiminished over his nine seasons. There were disappointments along the way, though, such as losing at the quarter-final stage in the Scottish Cup on three occasions and defeat in a B&Q cup final.

The one that got away was definitely the 1991 Scottish Cup quarter-final, when they outplayed eventual winners Motherwell over two matches, eventually losing on penalties. Rowan's last full season was one of the most memorable for him. Morton had been relegated to the second division at the end of season 1993–94, but bounced straight back as Champions the following season. Rowan's latest striking partner was the emerging Derek Lilley, and they struck up a formidable partnership with Rowan scoring some crucial goals. A victory over Dumbarton at Cappielow in the last match secured the championship.

We had recruited two excellent Finnish Internationals, Janne Lindberg and Marko Rajamaki, and they made all the difference. In the last match against Dumbarton they were outstanding, and helped propel us to the championship.

Another major factor in Morton's success that season was the form and leadership of Derek McInnes.

Derek was an outstanding player for us. He had leadership qualities at an early age. That was why Allan McGraw made him captain when he was barely 21. He took responsibility and was very consistent, and was an excellent leader and organiser. He wasn't afraid to change things on the park if it wasn't working. I remember Derek when he was 16 and just coming into the side. He absolutely oozed talent. And look at what he's achieved. He's had several bad injuries and come through with flying colours. Derek is an exceptional pro.

Once again Rowan was struck by the support and appreciation of the Morton fans, and this was reinforced over the next two years as Rowan's testimonial committee organised a series of functions culminating in a testimonial match against Falkirk that allowed the fans to display their affection and appreciation for a great servant. As season 1995–96 dawned, Rowan was 34. Some of the sharpness may have gone, and as he admits he was slowing down slightly, but the appetite was still there. Morton had signed Warren Hawke from Berwick Rangers, a similar type of player to Rowan, and it looked as if Allan McGraw's preferred striking partnership would be Lilley and Hawke.

I was sensible about the situation. I could read between the lines, but Allan was up front with me, and it was Allan that told me about Queen of the South's interest. It was a wrench to leave Morton. I had some great times there, and I knew my heart would never really leave the place that gave me enormous pleasure and satisfaction. I had played with some terrific players. Guys like Derek Lilley, Derek McInnes, Allan Mahood, Derek Collins, David Wylie, and many more. Players that you knew from an early age were going to make it. It was an honour to be involved with these players. It was an honour to play for Allan McGraw and Morton, and a particular highlight for me was a brief spell as captain. I knew the first time I walked through the gates that Cappielow was a special place. I made many close friends during my time at Morton, and I will never forget the kindness of the supporters. They gave me a lot of pleasure and hopefully I gave something back to them.

A new challenge beckoned for Rowan and he returned to his first senior club, Queen of the South. Taking over as player-manager in January 1996, Rowan and his assistant Mark Shanks set about restructuring the club. Rowan had witnessed first-hand under Allan McGraw the benefits of a successful youth policy, and he decided it was the route to follow at Queens. Rowan initiated a government-sponsored Skill Seekers programme at Queens, which soon bore fruit. Players such as Jamie McAllister, Chris Doug and David Lilley were all brought through the Skill Seekers Programme, and went on to bigger things with Aberdeen, Notts Forest and Partick Thistle, with McAllister winning international recognition. When Rowan took over at Queens they were 13 points adrift at the bottom of the second division, but by the end of the season he had kept them in the division. In his second season at Palmerston Queens reached the Challenge Cup Final and finished fourth in the second division. He was making slow, but sure progress, but the Queen's directors didn't share his vision and patience, and he was sacked three years to the day of his appointment. It is clearly something that still rankles with Rowan, as he feels there is still some unfinished business. However hard it may have been to take at the time, Rowan's sacking may well turn out to be the best thing that could have happened to him. As he says himself, 'my experience at Queens has made me stronger as a person and as a manager.'

Ironically, as a player Rowan had vowed never to move into management. As a player at Morton he saw the demands made on Allan McGraw, and the toll on his health, but as he admits himself, when the opportunity came up to manage a club, he couldn't resist. After a brief tenure coaching in Canada and America, Rowan landed the manager's post at Gretna FC, then in the Unibond First Division in England. 'When I arrived the place was a shambles and only six players turned up for the first training session.'

Rowan immediately instigated the Skill Seekers Programme at Gretna, and set his sights high. When, in 2002 the Scottish League expanded from 40 to 42 clubs, Gretna, with Rowan as the driving force, applied for membership. They were rewarded by being elected to the Scottish Third Division.

It was one of the greatest days of my life when I found out that we had won the vote. It was a culmination of three years hard work. And what set the whole thing off was when the fixtures were published for our first season in the League.

By season 2002–03 Morton had fallen from grace, and had narrowly escaped going bust after the disastrous tenure of chairman Hugh Scott. They had just been relegated to Scotland's lowest division. As Rowan says: 'I suppose it was fate when the computer drew Gretna and Morton together.'

Unbelievably, Gretna's first match in the Scottish League was against Morton at Raydale Park. Morton fans travelled down to Gretna in their droves as much to pay tribute to Rowan as to cheer on their side. On a baking hot summer's day the sides fought out a 1–1 draw, and Rowan, at the age of 41, but still registered as a player, couldn't resist naming himself as substitute. He received a tremendous ovation when he came on for the last 10 minutes of an emotional occasion.

Gretna easily consolidated their new found League status, finishing sixth, with Rowan making one other appearance as a player, and inevitably scoring, making him at 41 years and 168 days one of the oldest men to score a senior goal in Scotland. Season 2003–04 saw Gretna just missing out on promotion, finishing third, and Rowan is confident that they will be playing second division football in

2005. He takes great pride in everything that he has achieved at Gretna in such a short space of time. 'I have a chairman in Brooks Mileson who shares my drive and vision, and we have great ambitions for Gretna.'

Rowan has strong views on football in general, but in particular the condition of youth development in Scotland.

I feel that there is a certain amount of lip service paid to youth development in this country. We have exceptional coaching up to the age of 14, but we seem to lose our way in the age group 14 to 16. I don't think there's enough ex-players involved at this stage. We are fine at the small sided games, but when we move up to 11 a side, the kids can't grasp it.

Working for so long with Allan McGraw has obviously left its mark on Rowan as he believes the way ahead for Gretna and Scottish football in general is to invest in youth.

For too long our clubs, particularly the bigger ones, were too quick to take the easy option and bring in foreign players who were only here for one last pay day. If that money had been invested in youth perhaps we wouldn't have the massive gap between us and the rest of the world at international level.

Rowan speaks with some authority. He is a fully qualified coach, having passed all his SFA coaching badges, and hasn't spent 25 years in the game without forming strong opinions and good habits. The last word on Rowan goes to the man who signed him for Morton – Allan McGraw:

Rowan was one of my best signings. I always felt we had a chance with Rowan in the side. He never knew when he was beaten, and would battle right to the end. He was often up against taller and stronger opponents, but would often best them, and his ability in the air was tremendous. What I admired most about Rowan was his enthusiasm and dedication.

He had to travel up to Greenock from Dumfries for training, and I don't think he was ever late once. All in all, a tremendous professional.

Rowan seems destined to make as big an impact in the managerial side of the game as he did as a player, a player who will always be sure of a warm welcome from the fans who idolised him. To them he will always be 'Super Ro!'

Morton playing statistics: (League, League Cup, Scottish Cup)

Season	Appearances	Goals
1986–87	44 +1sub	26
1987–88	39	8
1988–89	37	14
1989–90	43	16
1990–91	39	8
1991–92	35	13
1992–93	32 +1sub	11
1993–94	39 +1sub	11
1994–95	31 +sub	10

Chapter 9

Derek McInnes
An Exceptional Player

It is often said that you only miss someone when they are no longer around. This is especially true in the case of Derek McInnes when one thinks back to the 1995–96 season. Morton were pushing hard for promotion to the Premier League, when midway through the season McInnes was sold to Rangers. Until then Morton had been worthy challengers, matching the more fancied Dunfermline and Dundee United stride for stride.

McInnes was the lynchpin of the side, but his departure broke up the best midfield in Division One. The transfer of McInnes, and Morton's failure to sign a similar type of player probably cost them promotion, and fuelled fans' suspicions that Morton lacked ambition, and were still too eager to sell their best players. The truth was more prosaic, as the manager of that exciting side Allan McGraw explains. 'Derek had watched so many of his teammates move on, and we had always said that if the right offer from a bigger side came in we wouldn't stand in his way.'

It is fair to say that for all Derek's importance to that Morton side, he was somewhat undervalued by a certain section of the Morton support. Indeed for a spell he was the target for the boo boys. But with Derek gone, Morton were forced to play defenders in his position, who, although good pros, lacked Derek's all-round qualities of composure, organisation and passing. When the season ended in a thrilling 2–2 draw at Cappielow with Dundee United in front of 14,000 fans with Morton just missing out on the play-offs, even Derek's sternest critic was forced to admit that he had been missed.

Derek McInnes was born in Paisley in 1971, and football was always a big factor in his life, thanks to his father who was a talented footballer. McInnes senior enjoyed a long career in junior football as a winger, and also had senior trials with St Johnstone and Dundee.

Derek's first club was Barrhead Boys Club, joining them at the tender age of nine. Derek spent many happy years there because as he says: 'A lot of good

Derek gets on his bike with some young fans along for the ride.

people ran the club, and I learned a lot there. It was a very well-run club, I was happy there and made a lot of good friends.'

A brief spell with Ferguslie United followed before he signed for Gleniffer Thistle Under-18s. Gleniffer had a good reputation for unearthing young talent, and consequently Gleniffer's matches were always well attended by senior scouts.

St Mirren were quite keen to take me, but John McMaster had heard my name from scouts and invited me down for a week's training during the school holidays, and I formed a really good relationship with him straight away. I think he saw something in me and thought I had a chance of making it, and I really enjoyed working with him from day one. I just had that gut feeling, and he was the main reason that I signed for Morton. It wasn't until a year later when I spoke to St Mirren manager Alex Smith and he told me that he couldn't believe I had knocked St Mirren back to go to Morton. But there had never been a concrete offer from St Mirren.

And so, not for the first time, Morton had stolen a promising young player from under their great rivals' noses. (think Jimmy Cowan and Billy Steel.) Derek joined the ground staff in October 1987 and made his debut in a youth game against Motherwell, scoring two goals.

As a result, he was swiftly promoted to the Premier League reserves the following week, again against Motherwell. When he signed for Morton Allan McGraw told Derek that if he was good enough he would get his chance in the first team, no matter how young he was. 'The gaffer was as good as his word, and I made my debut at 16.'

Derek did indeed make his debut at 16 against Dundee United and became part of an assembly line of talented youngsters nurtured by star-spotter McGraw. The good practices and habits he learned at Morton have stood Derek in good stead throughout his career.

I felt I progressed quite quickly. I was still playing for Gleniffer on a Saturday, training with Morton Monday to Friday and playing for the youth team. The season I signed for Morton, Gleniffer won the Scottish Cup, and when I made my first-team debut in April 1988, I was still a Gleniffer Thistle player. In fact, I played in the Under-18 Scottish Cup Final after I had played a couple of games in the Premier League.

Derek considers himself fortunate to have come under the tutelage of the legendary Allan McGraw. 'He obviously wasn't out on the training ground too much, but he gave you so much confidence. He had confidence in you, that you could do a job for him.'

Derek made his debut for Morton aged 16 against Dundee United at Cappielow as a second-half substitute, and played the full match the following week against Hibs. The *Greenock Telegraph* reporter was impressed with Derek against United and wrote: 'McInnes is highly regarded at Cappiclow and showed glimpses of promise in his half hour as substitute.'

Derek himself could be well pleased with his showing, and was unlucky not to score with a header after a well-timed run.

It was strange. On the morning of my debut I was doing my paper run and I was reading in the papers that I was about to make my debut. I had played a few reserve games and didn't feel out of my depth, and Allan McGraw and John McMaster had gradually introduced me into training with the first team, and I was travelling to away games with the first-team squad, but it was still a big, big shock when I got my chance. The team had already been relegated and some of the players knew they weren't getting kept on, but I had everything to play for. I enjoyed both games even though we lost them. I was up against John Collins at Easter Road, and I felt I did well, and I was disappointed that the season had finished. It was just beginning to happen for me though, and it gave me something to aim for the following season.

Derek McInnes in
full flow against
Dumbarton in May
1995. Morton won
the game 2–0.

From the following season Derek was more or less a regular as Allan McGraw set about rebuilding his side after a confidence-shattering season:

The good thing about Allan McGraw and a club like Morton was that he put you in even though you were far from the finished article. He allowed you to make your mistakes and learn the game. At first division level if he saw you were improving he was willing to be patient. Looking back now, I was raw and making wrong decisions, but I always felt I had the backing and the full belief of the boss and John McMaster who was pushing me all the time. When I signed for Morton I was told that if I progressed then I'd get a chance. A lot of clubs promise that but don't really follow it through, but Morton have always been known as a club that will give youngsters a chance. A lot of people see them as a selling club but that's a bit harsh. I see them as a club that gives boys a chance to develop, and I certainly got that chance. I was just delighted to get the chance to be a full-time footballer. I just loved everything about it. The young lads today don't know how lucky they are. We had to do everything from cutting the grass to cleaning the toilets, and we wouldn't get home till six o'clock at night. Even after my debut for the first-team John McMaster threw me a brush and told me to clean the dressing room. But I enjoyed all that. I was just so grateful to be involved with a professional club. I didn't mind the chores because I was just so glad to be in a football environment, and I wanted to make the most of the opportunity. I was picked up quite late at 16, and I appreciated it even more because of that.

Derek makes no secret of his admiration and respect for John McMaster and credits him as the major factor in his early career.

John taught me a lot of good habits and showed me how to act like a professional footballer on and off the park. John was brilliant at his job. The combination of him and Allan McGraw worked really well. He was

*very hands on and loved getting involved with training, and he put so
many hours in.*

*The boss because of his knees couldn't get too involved in training but
you always knew he was the boss, there was so much respect for him from
the most senior player right down to the ground staff boys. Come a
Saturday he was brilliant at motivating us, and getting the best out of
us. And on the Monday you would sit with him in his office, he would
pour you a cup of tea and sit with you for half an hour talking through
what he expected of you.*

Derek continued to improve under the wise tutelage of McGraw and McMaster
in a Morton side that played attacking, entertaining football. In his first full
season with Morton, still aged only 17, he played almost 30 games and suffered
an early Scottish Cup disappointment when Morton lost in a quarter-final replay
to St Johnstone, and so missed out on a chance of playing against Rangers in the
semi-final. The first St Johnstone match finished 2–2 at Cappielow, with 10-man
Morton also missing a penalty. As Derek admits, however, St Johnstone were the
better side in the replay and triumphed 3–2.

*It was a learning experience for me. I was up against Gary Thomson in
midfield, a hard, aggressive player, and in the end they were just too
good and experienced for us. The annoying thing was that we had beaten
them 1–0 at their ground a couple of weeks previously. What I remember
most about the replay was the tremendous Morton support, and that was
when I first realised what a great support Morton have.*

He did, however score his first goal for 'Ton that season against Falkirk at
Cappielow, a superb right-foot volley. Lightning was to strike twice when, in
season 1990–91 again in the Scottish Cup quarter-finals, Morton outplayed
eventual winners Motherwell over two matches before losing on penalties.
Derek was disappointed to be listed as substitute for both Motherwell matches.
Still only 19, his form had understandably dipped a little, and he only played

the last 10 minutes of extra time in the replay. As confident as ever, Derek slotted away Morton's first penalty, but was left frustrated as Morton eventually lost 5–4.

> *We outplayed Motherwell in the first game at Fir Park, and went into the replay with a lot of confidence, and really outplayed them again. Even in extra time we kept pushing forward trying to win the match. I look back on it as a missed opportunity, but I saw how much the Scottish Cup means to the town.*

On the field, Derek learned much from the wise old head of Iain MacDonald. Never a fans' favourite, MacDonald taught Derek how to look after himself in the often frenzied midfield that they both occupied.

> *Ian was a real gallus Glasgow guy with a real confidence about him. Even when he wasn't playing well, he talked himself up so much you believed that he actually had had a good game! He was a central midfielder like me, and he always thought I was a nice player but he thought I needed to learn to look after myself more. He taught me to be a bit more streetwise on the park. I also admired guys like Rowan Alexander and Jim Hunter who had a great work ethic. They were part-time but would come in after a hard shift and really put the effort in at training.*
>
> *They had a great appetite for the game and trained ever so hard all the time. They were probably the two most important players at Cappielow in my early days.*

Jim Hunter was the man that the legendary Brian Clough claimed he would have signed had he been three inches taller. Still a good friend of Derek's, Jim had to retire early through injury, but is fondly remembered at Cappielow as a scrupulously fair but hard-tackling defender who even impressed renowned Rangers' hardman Graham Roberts. The canny McGraw protected Derek as much as possible, at one stage playing him wide right in midfield away from the hurly burly of central midfield.

He was rewarded with Derek's best tally of goals for a season, as he pitched in with seven goals. Goalscoring, as Derek admits, has never been his strong point, and it is one of Derek's regrets that he hasn't scored more regularly throughout his career.

By the age of 21 Derek was one of Morton's most important players. So much so, that Allan McGraw didn't hesitate to make him captain at that early age. Perhaps Allan saw something in the young McInnes that other managers would see later on in his career. Upon signing for both West Bromich Albion and Dundee United, Derek was immediately installed as captain by managers Gary Megson and Ian McCall. Allan McGraw remembers the young McInnes as a tremendous asset to have at the club:

> Derek had a great attitude from day one at the club. I made him captain
> at 21, and he was a great skipper for me. At training the other players
> would take their lead from him, and if he was playing well, then the
> team would play well.

However, although Derek was improving as a player and Morton continued to play their trademark attacking football, Morton were unable to return to the Premier League.

> I felt that if we had just given it that bit extra push and signed another
> couple of players we could have made it back to the Premier. But we
> ended up selling Alex Mathie, Brian Reid and Alan Mahood, and I felt
> a bit aggrieved, and I felt the supporters' frustration. And from a personal
> point of view, I saw all these players going, and although I was delighted
> for them personally, I felt that if Morton weren't going to make that effort
> to get promoted, I wanted to better myself too.
>   The chairman [John Wilson] got a lot of stick at the time, but looking
> back he ran a really tight ship and he wouldn't allow Morton to get into
> any sort of trouble. He was always good to me and was a really good

McInnes and Stephen McCahill celebrate Morton's 2-0 win over Dumbarton to win the Second Division in 1995. It was all too much for Marko Rajmaki (background)!

man, and looking back, you can see his point of view but it was frustrating at the time.

Opportunities to move to Chelsea and QPR fell through as Morton held out for more money. Derek actually shook hands and agreed personal terms with Chelsea manager Ian Porterfield, and three weeks training at QPR with Les Ferdinand and Ray Wilkins among others resulted in Derek shaking hands on a £250,000 deal with QPR manager Gerry Francis. Both deals were scuppered when Morton asked for more money.

Although the Chelsea one would have been nice, I had really settled at QPR and I felt I could have done well, so it was a big blow. But looking back now when I went to Rangers I felt I was ready for it. I don't think I could have coped when I was 20 or 21.

Derek's frustration was compounded when he dislocated his kneecap against Brechin in October 1993. Seven months and two operations later Derek's knee was no better, and a make or break third operation was required.

I went down to Cambridge and the surgeon Mr Dandy whom I have a lot to thank for, told me that if the third operation didn't work then I could forget about a career in professional football. He carried out a procedure called a lateral release which lifted the kneecap up and set it again. I was out for nine or 10 months and Morton to their credit sent me to Lilleshall, and that really brought me back to fitness.

However, by this time Morton were in the second division. A horrendous injury list had resulted in relegation in season 1993–94. It was no coincidence that Derek missed most of that season. It was a depressing time for Derek, but he gives due credit to Morton for his recovery. It was during his spell on the sidelines that Derek took a job with the Post Office. 'I really enjoyed working there, but it gave me the impetus to give football one last big effort.'

Derek holds the
Second Division
Trophy aloft in 1995.

A fully fit Derek returned to a Morton side in October 1994 bolstered by the signings of the two Finns Janne Lindberg and Marko Rajamaki. His first match back after his injury was away to Berwick.

I had one reserve game under my belt, and to be honest wasn't 100% confident. By then Peter Cormack had been appointed the gaffer's assistant, and I wanted to prove myself to him. But it was a big step after being out for so long and I had some reservations. But I played well and we won 2–1. It was a relief to get through the game, but Lindberg, Rajamaki and Hawke had added a freshness to the team, and we never looked back after that match. It was the start of my best spell of football for Morton. I felt I came back a different type of player. All the gym work had paid off and I was stronger, fitter, and more aggressive.

With Warren Hawke up front benefiting from Derek's promptings Morton won the second division at a canter, and Derek crowned his comeback with the second division player of the year award. Derek credits Janne Lindberg with the final stage in his development as a Morton player.

Janne brought a new level of professionalism to Cappielow. I really enjoyed playing with him, and watching him in training. When I was working my way back to fitness after my knee injury I saw first-hand how hard he worked in the gym and in training. He didn't do it for effect. He did it because he was a tremendous professional, and a lot of it rubbed off on me.

Season 1995–96 saw Morton carry on the previous season's momentum. With a hugely influential McInnes pulling the strings in midfield Morton were never out of the top three in the first dozen games of the season as they more than matched their more fancied rivals Dunfermline and Dundee United.

With Warren Hawke and Derek Lilley up front and the best midfield in the division of Lindberg, Mahood and McInnes, it looked as if Derek would achieve his ambition of playing with Morton in the Premier League. An early season League Cup tie at Ibrox saw Derek pitched against Paul Gascoigne in one of his first games for Rangers. 'We went into the match confident we could get a favourable result, and it was an opportunity for me to show what I could do.'

As ever, a tremendous 'Ton support cheered the side on, but although not disgraced Morton lost 3–0. Derek, however, had an excellent match and gained some notoriety as one of the first players in Scotland to be on the receiving end of Gazza's flying elbows. 'I told him during the game that he was out of order, and had a couple of digs back at him, but it was all forgotten about after the match.' Indeed it was, as Derek explains:

About six months after I signed for Rangers Gazza told me that immediately after the cup match he had told Walter Smith that he should sign me. He reckoned I was a good short passer, a good long passer, and could give as good as I got. Oh yes, and he reckoned I was a mouthy little so and so as well!

Walter Smith already knew all about Derek however, as he had had Derek watched in every match that season. Derek's form had not gone unnoticed. Several top sides north and south of the Border made bids for Derek, but once Rangers made their interest known, there was no contest for Derek. The McInnes transfer saga is a good example of the wheeling and dealing that goes on without the fans' knowledge.

After my injury, rather than sign for another year I took a chance and let my contract run down, and by the time we won the second division, my contract was due to run out in the summer.

So the transfer would have gone to a tribunal and Morton would have got virtually nothing for me, which I didn't want. I wanted the club to get something for me. To be honest I didn't really want to leave at that time, I was really enjoying my football and I felt that we had a side that would have won the first division and gone up to the Premier, which would have satisfied me. Morton then made me an offer that really pushed the boat out for them, and I felt obliged to have another year with Morton. I wanted to play in the Premier and I thought Morton could make it, so I was more than happy to sign another year's contract with the provision that there was a clause that if an offer of x amount came in matching an agreed figure, then it would give me the decision to move or not.

Derek was by now a hot property and a bidding war took place as several English and Scottish Premier sides made bids for his services. But then Rangers entered the fray, and a war of words broke out between Morton chairman John Wilson and Derek's agent. John Wilson accused the agent of a breach of confidence regarding the clause in Derek's contract.

He was severely miffed that Rangers had come in with a bid well below the other clubs, and felt that the agent might have alerted them to the clause without Derek's knowledge. John Wilson felt that Derek was a future international and was in no mood to let him go cheaply, but Morton finally recognised that Derek, as a loyal servant, deserved the chance to play for the club he had supported as a boy. A fee of £260,000 as stipulated in the agreement saw Derek move to Ibrox. His last game was against Dundee at Dens Park in November 1995.

I always remember the reception I got from the fans. It had been in the press that I was signing for Rangers the following Monday and it was my last game, and they could easily have turned on me, but to a man they sang my name and clapped me off the park which meant a lot to me. I would have hated to have left with bad feeling, but I think I left with the best wishes of everyone. The one thing that annoyed me was I thought Morton were going to be promoted and I wanted to be part of that, but I felt as if I was ready for a club like Rangers. I felt that if I had knocked them back I would have regretted it for the rest of my career.

The match against Rangers in August 1995 that sealed Derek McInnes's transfer to the club. The Rangers players in the picture are David Robertson (left) and Paul Gascoigne (right).

Derek had been a Morton regular for eight years and left with many happy memories of his time there. He had a second division winners' medal along with the aforementioned player of the year award, and had won a clutch of supporters' awards.

He had experienced the disappointment of losing the B&Q Cup Final, and in common with many fine Morton players of the past and present had been overlooked for international honours. He was named in an Under-21 pool, only for the SFA to discover he was too old. Looking back, it's hard to believe that Derek was overlooked for international honours at all levels until he was 31. But he left Cappielow with an appreciation of everything Morton had done for him and grateful that he had been given the chance to be a professional footballer. Morton had also gained a fan as Derek's father, although a Rangers supporter, had taken to watching all of Derek's matches home and away. 'My dad loved going to Morton matches and he made a lot of friends.'

Unfortunately, a cruciate injury hampered Derek's progress in his first season at Rangers, although he recovered to play a part in Rangers' nine in a row season. Derek enjoyed working under Walter Smith, and saw first-hand the difference between managing a provincial club like Morton and a huge club like Rangers. The arrival of Dick Advocat gave Derek a different insight into club management. Suffice to say that Derek does not rate Advocat's man management skills too highly.

Towards the end of Derek's time at Rangers, he felt that Advocat only played him when others weren't available, although he did play a major part in Rangers' treble in Advocat's first season. A three-month loan spell with Stockport under Gary Megson got Derek fit and playing again. When Derek returned to Rangers, however, he realised that he wasn't included in Dick Advocat's future plans, and a £500,000 move to Toulouse in France soon followed. Derek's spell there was hampered by injury, but he enjoyed the experience, and saw first-hand the excellent infrastructure that has resulted in the success that France has enjoyed over the last decade at club and international level. In 1999 Gary Megson became manager of West Bromwich Albion, and made Derek one of his first signings. Megson obviously saw something in Derek that had prompted Allan McGraw to make him skipper at 21, because he appointed Derek his captain in Derek's very first match. Finding in Megson a kindred spirit, Derek blossomed and led West Brom to the Premiership, and even won belated international recognition, winning two caps at the age of 31.

But by 2003 Derek and his family had a hankering to return to Scotland, and West Brom reluctantly allowed him to move to Dundee United. Manager Ian

McCall immediately installed Derek as captain as he set about rejuvenating United.

Now aged 33, and having learned how to look after his body with sensible eating and training programmes, Derek feels he can play at the top level until he is 35 at least, citing Stuart McCall as an example. When he finishes with the playing side, Derek would like to stay in the game in some capacity and has gained some coaching certificates. And the news for Morton fans is good, because as he says 'I have so many great memories of Morton and I know it sounds corny, but I really would like to end my career back at Morton. After all, if I hadn't met Allan McGraw and John McMaster when I did, I might not have got the chance to be a professional footballer.'

That is all in the future, but Derek does give the impression that he has some unfinished business at Cappielow. He believes the club are heading back to the big-time after almost going out of business.

Talking to Derek, one is left with the clear impression that he is not one of the modern-day breed of footballers who is happy just to take, take, take, and give nothing back to the game.

He concedes that he was not naturally gifted and had to work very hard to succeed in the game. He has had many ups and downs in his career, with several injuries, and his early exit from Rangers.

When I left Rangers I was determined to prove that it wasn't necessarily downhill for me. That's why Gary Megson was the right manager for me at the right time as he shares my drive and ambition. Equally, I want to show the Dundee United fans that I'm not just here to pick up the money and see out my career.

Derek now seems to have achieved the status that perhaps eluded him at Morton. He was recently voted the club's third-greatest player of all time, something this modest man would find overwhelming. Perhaps Arthur Montford should have the last word on Derek McInnes.

I always felt that Derek had those qualities belonging to exceptional players – to find time on the ball, never seemed rushed, and always knowing what to do with the ball when he got it. Derek was never a prolific goal scorer, but one goal in particular stands out against Stirling Albion from at least 30 yards. One of the top dozen Morton goals I have seen. I was sorry and surprised he didn't fit into the Rangers pattern of play, but I am delighted he is now doing what he does best – organising, finding time on the ball and using it well. And a particularly nice young man into the bargain.

Morton playing statistics: (League, League Cup, Scottish Cup)

Season	Appearances	Goals
1987–88	2 subs	0
1988–89	30 + 5 subs	1
1989–90	15 + 11 subs	1
1990–91	25 + 7 subs	3
1991–92	41 + 4 subs	7
1992–93	42 + 1 sub	2
1993–94	17	1
1994–95	27	3
1995–96	13	1

Chapter 10

Derek Collins
Mr Consistency

One of the unwritten laws in football is that it never works second time around when a popular player goes back to the club where he made his name. Think back to the likes of Derek Johnstone, a hero at Rangers first time around, but when he went back to Ibrox after a spell in England, it just wasn't the same. Derek Collins is very much the exception to that rule. Derek made his name as a skilful full-back over 12 seasons at Cappielow before leaving to further his career. Fast forward to 2001, when Morton had come back from the brink of extinction, and Derek had come to the end of his time at Hibernian. A patchwork side was thrown together, basically to enable Morton to fulfill their fixtures. The club needed all the loyal servants they could muster and Derek was a logical choice. It was as if he had never been away.

It's very easy to apply clichés to Derek Collins. As a young player he most certainly was 'an old head on young shoulders.' Throughout his career he has undoubtedly been 'Mr Consistency' but what about 'loyal servant'? Because there is no doubting Derek's loyalty and commitment to Morton Football Club. As Derek says about his choice to return to Morton in 2001: 'I had other offers on the table. But I felt going back to Morton was a chance for me to give something back to the club that had been so good to me over the years.'

Derek Collins was born in Glasgow in 1969, and with an elder brother who was a keen footballer, and an uncle, Dennis Hollywood, who had played for Southampton in the 1960s and 1970s, football was a constant factor in his life. Derek's formative years were spent playing for his school in Glasgow, and juvenile side Renfrew Waverley, with whom he won the Scottish Cup at Under-16 and Under-18 levels. Derek is very appreciative of his time with the Waverley. 'I received a good education there. The coaching was top class and Renfrew Waverley gave me a solid grounding for the future.'

It was while playing with Renfrew Waverley at Cappielow against a Morton Under-18s side that Derek caught the eye of Morton scout George Gillespie, and he was invited down to Cappielow for trials. Manager Allan McGraw ran an eye over Derek and wasted no time in signing him in July 1987. For Derek, it was an easy choice to make. On the face of it, it was a good time to join Morton, as they had just won promotion back to the Premier League. The legendary Allan McGraw was in charge, and they had a good coach in John McMaster. Derek became a full-time player in July 1987. 'I jumped at the chance. There was no second thoughts about it. I knew it was a fantastic opportunity.'

Derek already knew a fair bit about Morton as he had attended a few derbies against St Mirren, as one of his coaches at Renfrew Waverley was – whisper it – a St Mirren fan.

As with all his young players, Allan McGraw promised Derek a first-team chance if he made the right progress, and Derek didn't have to wait too long for that chance. After a couple of reserve-team matches, Derek was handed his first-team debut against Motherwell in October 1987 at right-back. His immediate opponent was tricky winger John Gahagan, who would later become Derek's teammate at Morton. John became well known as an after dinner speaker when he hung up his boots, and, obviously with tongue firmly in cheek, later nominated Derek as his hardest opponent. The match ended 1–1, and Derek received favourable reviews for a calm, mature performance. He had stepped straight out of Under-18 football into the Premier League, and didn't look out of place at all.

It was probably the youthful innocence if you like. There was no fear because I was young and didn't really have any worries because it was just another game to me, and I just wanted to be playing football. I didn't feel any pressure, I just went out and enjoyed the game. It just seemed a natural step up for me.

But Morton were already finding the demands of the Premier League too much for them, and were relegated at the end of the season. Derek had nonetheless proved to be the find of the season, and had made such an impression that there was already interest from bigger clubs including both Celtic and Rangers. In fact, Celtic did make a bid for Derek, but were given no encouragement by Morton. One high spot of the season was a rare victory over Graeme Souness's Rangers at Cappielow. It was Morton's first league victory at Cappielow over Rangers for almost 70 years. Derek scored his first goal for the club, after a foray into nose bleed territory ended with a 35-yard swerving cross shot that eluded 'Gers 'keeper Chris Woods. The goal set Morton on their way, and sent Souness searching for the tea cups.

Against Rangers, and in several other games that season, Derek operated in midfield, a position he was comfortable with, due to his all-round composure and attacking instincts. He would return periodically to midfield throughout his career, but Morton fans were happy that the problem right-back position, which had never been satisfactorily filled since the departure of fans' favourite Davie Hayes, now looked in safe hands. Derek's progress was one of the few high spots of that season for Morton. Putting aside the disappointment of relegation, it had been an excellent debut season for Derek with 30 games under his belt at the age of 18. He also had the pleasure of playing alongside another long-serving Cappielow favourite, Jim Holmes. When Derek is asked who he learned most from as a young player he has no hesitation.

I have to say Jim Holmes was probably my biggest influence as a young player. Homer was a pure footballer. Watching him I decided that was the way to go. Fans like to see full backs clattering wingers and coming out with the ball, but that was never a big part of my game. Homer could handle himself as well, but everything about him was football. He was a fantastic footballer, and he definitely influenced my approach to the game.

For Allan McGraw though, it was blatantly obvious that Morton's only hope lay in the development of youth. 16-year-old Derek McInnes was introduced to first-team action in 1988, and in the next few seasons, talented youngsters such as David Hopkin, Allan Mahood, and Derek Lilley would join the other two Dereks in the first team. Unsurprisingly, Derek is a big fan of Allan McGraw.

A big part of modern day football is man management, and Allan McGraw excelled in that area. That was one of his strengths. He knew how to deal with individuals. Whereas in those days it was very much the old school of management with the tea cups and the hair dryer, Allan was the opposite, he would sit you down and talk things through.

Former centre-half George Anderson was also a big help to Derek in the early stages of his career, as Derek remembers:

George Anderson was coaching at Morton after he had retired as a player, and he helped me a lot in the early days. He was very much of the old school, and he took me under his wing a bit. I was very laid back and quiet, and George helped to boost my confidence by telling me I was a good player, and wouldn't be at Cappielow if I wasn't.

Derek only missed three matches the following season as he continued to establish his credentials as one of Morton's most promising players. He endured the disappointment of a Scottish Cup quarter-final exit against St Johnstone, in a tie that Morton really should have won, and Morton finished the season fifth. As the 1990s dawned, the club's aim was very much Premier League football, but while they always produced attacking, attractive football, too often Morton underachieved in the league, partly due to the policy of selling on their best players. Did Derek ever get frustrated at the constant stream of young footballers moving on to bigger and better things?

I had been given the standard Morton promise that if I did well I could move on if the right offer came in, and through the course of time there was interest from English clubs, but I think for clubs in general it's sometimes in their best interest to let some players go, and keep others for the sake of the team. I was very much a team player and the club knew that. There is a bit of give and take. They can feed you enough information, like telling you that there's a big club interested, just keep playing the way you are, type of thing, but at the same time just enough to keep you at the club.

Perhaps Derek has given us an insight into the famous McGraw man management!

Morton's best performances in the early nineties were in the cup competitions including two memorable Scottish Cup quarter-final matches against eventual winners, Premier League Motherwell. Morton eventually lost on penalties, but Derek has fond memories of the matches as he was directly up against the late Davie Cooper. One downside of staying at the one club for so long is the danger of going stale, and Derek does admit that at one stage this was a danger as week in week out he was facing the same opponents on the same grounds.

There have, of course, been some great characters at Cappielow during Derek's time at the club.

Dougie Robertson was funny guy, and John Boag was something else! Mark Pickering was a cracker too, the only guy I know who would deliberately take a bad touch so that he could kick his opponent with the second! And the least said about Rowan Alexander's sartorial elegance the better. He was still wearing a herringbone jacket in the nineties, and his hair always looked as if it had been blown dry in a wind tunnel! Jim Hunter was one of the stand-out players in all my time at Cappielow. If it hadn't been for his injury he could have become one of the best defenders in the Scottish game. There wasn't much of him, but he was one of the hardest but fairest players in the game.

Morton were relegated to the second division in season 1993–94, and it was obvious that investment was required. Two high-quality Finnish players, Janne Lindberg and Marko Rajamaki, were brought to Cappielow, and made a huge impression there. Derek concurs with Derek McInnes in his opinion of Janne Lindberg.

To say he was a good player is a major understatement. I don't ever remember him ever giving the ball away. He just brought a real professionalism into the club. He had an incredible influence on the club. He was immense over the three seasons I played with him. Definitely one of the best players I have ever played with. The midfield we had at that time was tremendous. And as good as Janne was that season, I actually thought that Derek McInnes even excelled him on occasions. The midfield was the driving force of that side and helped propel us to the title.

So, after one season in the second division, Morton won promotion back to the first as champions. But they weren't prepared to just make up the numbers. The first match of the season found them away to Dundee United who had just been relegated from the Premier League for the first time in their history. A 1–1 draw established Morton's credentials as promotion contenders, and they continued to play their open, attractive football. The transfer of McInnes to Rangers in November 1995 could have derailed their season, but Allan McGraw and Peter Cormack masterfully regrouped the side to keep 'Ton in the promotion race. The final match of the season saw 14,000 fans pack Cappielow to the rafters. There were many permutations involving Morton, Dundee United and Dunfermline, and if Morton had won and the Pars had lost, 'Ton would have gone up to the Premier as champions. An emotional rollercoaster of a match ended in a 2–2 draw and with Dunfermline winning, Morton finished in third place and just missed the play-offs on goal difference. Derek says:

> *I believe strongly in momentum in football, and we had just come off the back of a successful season and were flying. We had a real belief in the team, it was almost as if we couldn't be beaten. We had great team spirit, and battling qualities, and we played good football. Certain games cost us in the end, but we were only one goal off a play-off position.*

Almost inevitably the following season 1996–97 was an anticlimax, and Morton finished a disappointing eighth, just above the relegation places. 1997–98 saw some improvement with a mid-table finish, but by then Morton had a new owner. 'Businessman' Hugh Scott had bought the club in 1997, and announced grand plans for a new stadium and funds to improve the team. New players were brought in, but there were early warning signs when Allan McGraw left the club, and players like Allan Mahood were allowed to leave for nothing. There was eventually a player exodus, and Derek was one of many who followed Derek Lilley, who moved to Leeds for £500,000, out the door.

> *I had a year left on my contract, and initially I was told that I would get an extension, but there was so many clauses attached that I felt my only option was to move on. I felt that I was forced out to be honest, and I left with a bitter taste.*

As a senior player at the club Derek felt duty bound to speak out against Hugh Scott's Machiavellian methods, and this led to some heated exchanges between the two. Derek eventually moved on to Hibernian in 1999 for £100,000, and could only watch aghast as events at Cappielow under Hugh Scott continued on a downward and depressing spiral.

541 appearances, having beaten David Wylie's existing record of 536 matches.

Although the move worked out great for me personally, I was still living in the area and I was aware of a lot of the negative stuff that was happening with the club. It was hard to talk with the supporters and listen to them telling me that the club was dying.

Derek enjoyed his two seasons at Easter Road under Alex McLeish, winning a Division One championship medal in his first season, and he enjoyed his return to the Premier League more than a decade after he had first played there. Falling out of favour at Hibs, he then moved to Partick Thistle on loan, and played a dozen matches in their successful Division Two title campaign.

It was a great experience working with John Lambie. I had been given all the warnings – you'll hate him, you won't get on – all that, but I had a great relationship with him. He was brilliant to work for, and a fantastic man manager, just like Allan McGraw.

Derek's next port of call was Preston in 2001, managed by David Moyes. Although he didn't play, he was kept involved by Moyes as Preston strived to achieve promotion to the Premiership. 'I was only there as cover for Graeme Alexander, but it was nice to be involved with a great club like Preston, and David Moyes told me that it was Dick Advocat who had recommended me to him.' In fact, Advocat had been hugely impressed by Derek in matches for Hibs against Rangers, and had indeed put his name forward to Moyes. After his spell at Preston, and a short spell in Malta, Derek was keen to be playing first-team football again. He had been watching the situation at Cappielow with increasing anger and alarm.

Derek Collins in action for Morton against Clydebank in 1996.

By 2001, Morton were in dire straits. Under the ownership of Hugh Scott, they had gradually gone into a downward spiral, and in 2001 were forced into administration. The fans rallied round and saved the club in the short term, but things still looked bleak until at almost the last gasp Douglas Rae stepped in and bought Hugh Scott's shareholding. But he had bought a club with no strips, virtually no players, a decrepit ground, and a mountain of debt. A new manager, Peter Cormack, was appointed, and a side hastily assembled.

'I had great memories of the club, and I wanted to help bring the good times back. I also saw it as my role to help give the club its good name back.' Derek's genuine love for the club is evident when he thinks back to the dark days of 2001.

> Over the years I had obviously established a strong bond with the club and the fans. There's just something about Morton Football Club, I couldn't imagine it not being here. And the supporters played such a huge part in saving the club. They deserve success.
>
> I had always had a good relationship with Douglas Rae, and I felt coming back at that time showed a bit of loyalty and gave me a chance to put something back into the club that had given me so much out of the game.

On an emotional day Morton took the field at Cappielow for their first match under the new regime in the second division with Derek as skipper. The fans were as good as a 12th man, as they virtually willed Morton to victory, 4–1 against Stenhousemuir. But Derek knew it would be a long hard season, and he was proved right when the makeshift side was relegated to the third division in May 2002. It was Morton's lowest ebb since they had propped up the old second division in 1961.

The only way was up, but a third of the way through season 2002–03, Morton sat fifth in the League, and were underachieving. A decision had to be made, and manager McPherson was sacked. Old hand John McCormack was brought in with the express instruction to win promotion. McCormack was just the type of manager required to drag a club up by its boot strings, and he made an immediate improvement. However, with six matches left, Morton lost a vital match against Albion Rovers, and promotion looked a forlorn hope. But suddenly everything gelled, and in a memorable spell, 'Ton won their last five matches without conceding a goal, and scored 12 in the process. There just seemed an inevitability about the whole thing, as everything came down to the last match of the season at home to Peterhead. Depending on which way the results went any two from Morton, Peterhead, East Fife and Albion Rovers could go up, and any one of the four could win the League. 8,490 fans turned up at Cappielow against Peterhead, proving once again how much the people of Inverclyde crave a successful Morton side. It was a nerve-wracking match, and no classic, with a single goal from Scott Bannerman sealing victory and the title for 'Ton. Derek is keen to give credit where it is due and he is keen to praise the Morton fans' contribution to 'Ton's title success.

The fans made a great contribution, especially at the away games when we were taking 1000 plus with us. Sometimes supporters don't realise the impact they can have on the team. They can dictate how a team can play. If the team doesn't start well and the fans get behind them and encourage them, then the players will react to that. It's amazing how big a part they can play, and in the Peterhead game they certainly played their part.

Derek considers season 2002–03 his most memorable in football, but if there was ever any doubt about the precarious nature of the life of a footballer, then the past two seasons of Derek Collins's career aptly demonstrate the highs and lows that are the very nature of football. After winning promotion back to the second division, the Morton players received deserved plaudits for their efforts. They then continued that momentum for the first half of season 2003–04, with a brand of football not seen at Cappielow since the days of McInnes, Mahood and Lindberg. They swept aside all comers in the League, and the 6–1 demolition of Airdrie United in November 2003 will live long in the memories of those who witnessed it. At one stage Morton were 13 points clear at the top, but come the New Year there was a slight dip in form, nothing too worrying at first, but a comprehensive Scottish Cup defeat by Premier League Partick Thistle showed up deficiencies in the team that gradually other sides began to exploit.

Gradually, 'Ton's massive lead began to be eroded, and their confidence began to evaporate. Only one of their last 10 games was won, and they lost their last four matches. In the end, they missed out on the promotion that at one stage looked a certainty. It was a chastening experience, and some of the fans dished out a fair amount of abuse. But on the whole, as Derek says, the Cappielow faithful demonstrated their legendary loyalty. It shows nothing can be taken for granted in football, and has ensured that Derek is doubly determined to make it up to the fans and win promotion in 2005. But, at 35, how long does Derek think he can play on?

I've been lucky with injuries over the years, and if I can stay clear of injury, I think I can play for another three years. Having said that, no one needs to tell you when your number's up. I'd like to finish on a high, I don't think there's any point in flogging yourself just to keep playing for the sake of it, but more and more players are playing on into their late thirties. As I get older I tend to tailor the type of training I do. I now let my head rule my heart. I now realise I'm not as fast as I was when I was 21.

Since his return to Cappielow, Derek has been operating in a sweeper role, a position many observers have long thought to be his best. Playing as the spare man at the back utilises his keen positional sense and ability to read the game, and will undoubtedly prolong his career. His days as a wing back, or the 'graveyard shift' as it is known, appear to be over, although Derek says he is still fit enough to handle the role. 'I would have to say that playing wing-back was my favourite position. It suited me to a tee because of my level of fitness.'

Unfortunately, Derek suffered one of his rare injuries last season when he was out of action for several weeks with ligament damage. Such was his importance to the team that he also played a substantial number of games when he was clearly not fully fit. 'The supporters knew it wasn't the real Derek Collins they saw last season, but I would never use injuries as an excuse for lack of form. Once you declare yourself fit and cross that white line, you accept all responsibility.'

Despite the disappointment of losing out on promotion in 2004, and Derek describes it as his worst experience in football, there was one bright spot for Derek in an otherwise topsy-turvy season. In a match against Airdrie in September 2003, Derek became Morton's record appearance holder when he passed the existing record of 536 held by former teammate goalkeeper David Wylie. It is a record that in the present football environment is unlikely to be broken. It remains to be seen what Derek's eventual total will be. At the end of 2003–04 the total stood at 564, and he is now on course to break the 600 barrier.

Derek is desperate to make up for the disappointent of last season by giving the fans first division football in 2005.

> *Hopefully we have recovered from last season's disappointment. We have a fairly young side and we can only learn from it. We can learn more from the hard times than when everything's going smoothly. It's easy when the weather's good, and the parks are nice, and we can play pretty football, but its when thing are going badly, that's when you need everybody to pull together, including the supporters.*

Allan McGraw signed Derek for Morton and worked with him for 10 years, and is still a big admirer.

> *It's easy to say it, but Derek is a great pro. He may have been a little quiet at times, but his ability was tremendous. He was another guy who was a great trainer and led by example. He was excellent going forward, very skilful, but that shouldn't detract from his defensive capabilities. He may not have been the hardest tackler, but that didn't matter because his*

timing was excellent. I always thought that if Derek had got his move a little earlier he could have gone even farther in the game.

There has always been a great team spirit at Cappielow, and players from all eras like to keep in touch with one another. Rowan Alexander for one makes a point of contacting old teammates like Derek Collins. The pair played together for the best part of 10 years at Morton and although they give each other endless good-natured stick, the respect is clear for all to see. Rowan says of Derek:

Derek sums up what a club like Morton is all about. He has tremendous loyalty and love for the club. When he was a young player he was very courteous and respectful towards senior figures at the club and now he is very much in that position himself. He was another who was very fit, he

Derek Collins with the Renfrewshire Cup after defeating St Mirren in 2003.

looked after himself very well and has benefited with a long and successful career. He was a fine captain and a pleasure to play with.

It is fair to say that possibly Derck has stayed too long at Cappielow. Perhaps if he had won a move to a bigger club and a higher stage like so many of his compatriots he would have gone further in the game. But he has no regrets. He has had a great career playing for a club whose supporters have taken him to their hearts. He has played with and against some great players, and considers himself fortunate to have had a man like Allan McGraw as his boss. He seems destined to be forever known as Morton's record appearance holder, and a Morton Great, and that's not bad for a guy who once stood in the St Mirren end of a Renfrewshire derby!

Morton playing statistics: (League, League Cup, Scottish Cup)

Season	Appearances	Goals
1987–88	29	1
1988–89	42	1
1989–90	41 +2sub	0
1990–91	41 +1sub	2
1991–92	49	1
1992–93	43	0
1993–94	38 +2sub	1
1994–95	38	1
1995–96	39	1
1996–97	42	0
1997–98	37	3
1998–99	19	0
2001–02	34	0
2002–03	40	0
2003–04	32	1